ONE NIGHT STAND & OTHER POEMS

JACK SPICER

ONE NIGHT STAND
&
OTHER POEMS

With a Preface by Robert Duncan

Edited by Donald Allen

Grey Fox Press
San Francisco

LIBRARY OF CONGRESS CATALOGING IN PUBLICATION DATA:

Spicer, Jack.
    One night stand & other poems.

    Includes index.
    I. Allen, Donald Merriam, 1912–   II. Title.
PS3569.P4705   811'.54   79-28053
ISBN 0-912516-45-3
ISBN 0-912516-46-1 pbk.

CONTENTS

PREFACE

With his first publisht poems in *Occident* (the student literary magazine of the University of California at Berkeley) in 1946 and in *Contour 1* in 1947, Jack Spicer's voice, at once humorous and painful, in which his delight in nonsense and his fear of nonsense meld, is already there. "The Bridge Game" and "The Chess Game" project his governing poetic fate; that is to say he took them seriously and he would follow through to the end of their series. He read language as he read cards or the plays in baseball as signs. Robin Blaser tells us in his terminal essay to *The Collected Books of Jack Spicer* that Spicer's last words were "My vocabulary did this to me" —words out of the misery of a terminal alcoholic coma. It seems true indeed that he died of a disease of the language game. Bridge, Chess, Pinball, the great American spectator sports Football and Baseball, and language, produced messages: sportscasts relayd binds and double-binds. In this sense of the death-throes underlying life, of the rules of the game, he was throughout an original of such power in my own imagination as a poet that whole areas of my creative consciousness still seem to me to have to do with a matter that was ultimately from him. His wit and his fine critical intelligence from the beginning are sharpend and exercised in a neverending battle against the autistic drive of the poem for him. And as with all autistic systems, his work haunts surrounding poetries. Those of us who knew him, and "we" must include all readers, for what he askt of us again and again was that we read him, carry with us his sting—the sting of the gadfly he so often in early days claimd to be—his wry dissent in the midst of sweetness, for again and again he knew the honey of Apollo to be bitter. In the end the fury could break loose, and the tyranny he sufferd in the courses of the poem would be inflicted upon his followers and readers. When I first met him in the Summer of 1946, he wanted to know first of all what I might know of the German poet Stefan George and his circle. The volume *Poems* with its introductory essay by Ernst Morwitz had been publisht in 1943, where—Spicer was right—I too had read the legend of the cult of Maximin, where a young boy in his death is enshrined in poetry that is also the heart of the poet. But there were also stories one heard of George's tyrannical hold on his followers. "To find an adequate expression for the pain of loneliness, is the problem of this book," Morwitz tells us of George's *Hymns,* "in which the poet turns his disappointment over a friendship that did not mature into rhythms of torment and regret." What is striking in Spicer's searching for what lay back of George's legend is not that George would ever be, as Rilke was, a model of the poet for Spicer, but that he was searching for his own self in poetry yet to be. The art was to be Orphic. Orpheus would be the tutelary daemon of Spicer's poetry: Orpheus, the Singer, yes. "The proudest boast made about Orpheus," Spicer wrote in a symposium on "The Poet and Poetry" in *Occident* in 1949 [see page 90] :

> was not that his poems were beautiful in and of themselves. There were no New Critics then. The proudest boast was that he, the singer with the songs, moved impossible audiences—trees, wild animals, the king of hell himself.

And it was Orpheus, the bereft Lover: the Spicer of these early poems was at war with the doctrines of the New Criticism that would see the poem as a thing in itself. In the course of *After Lorca* he would himself come to face the specter of the text in Poetry, and in the book *Language,* which I read as I read all Spicer's work in the spirit of his poems from the beginning, a new generation of poets after his death would read the crisis of an old poetry of reference and passion in which the directive to a New Criticism and its Poetry, again demanding that reference be stript away, is given. But the Spicer of 1949 was determined that the poem was voice:

They have taken poetry (already removed from its main source of interest—the human voice) and have completed the job of denuding it of any remaining connection with person, place and time. What is left is proudly exhibited in their essays—the dull horror of naked, pure poetry.

A Singer of Love Song. At the end in 1965 there will be that song: "The dark / forest of words lets in some light from its branches. / Mocking them, the deep leaves / That time leaves us / Words, loves." *(Language)* and *(Book of Magazine Verse)* "What is important is what we don't kill each other with / And a loving hand reaches a loving hand." "Words, loves" the despairing of words, the dis-pairing of loves: in those last "words" after "My vocabulary did this to me," he said, so Robin Blaser remembers his legacy: "Your love will let you go on." That "you" is beautiful, for it is not only immediate and personal, so that Blaser emerges as the chosen disciple as John (Jack's baptismal name) emerges in the gnostic *Acts of John*; but it is also plural—it blesses all who answer to its declaration. For the Orpheus-Poet that Spicer came to be was not only the Singer of Love but the Hero who entering Hell returns and in the rite of passage loses his Beloved to sing of unrequited love, of Love in Search: he is the Leader of a Circle of those who follow his Song—"impossible audiences."

It makes us wonder, this Master of Song's Magic whom we heard of long ago in childhood fairytale, where Persephone may have been also the Queen Under the Hill, and Eurydice, a changeling sylph, a shadowy love slipping back from the light of day and our wakening search, back into the shadowworld, her own element. In these early poems, "Orpheus After Eurydice," "Orpheus in Hell," "Orpheus' Song to Apollo," "A Night in Four Parts," and "The Song of the Bird in the Loins" speak from this mask—Spicer in the period of these poems immersed in the study of Yeats would have so used the word "mask": it would verge upon the Hallowe'en mask—he could identify with Jack Pumpkinhead in *The Land of Oz*. Just as the Orphic mystery Master of Song was always in part the story hero of a Wonder Tale, so mystery cult and wonder story were stage figures. It is part of the travesty of theater that we find Eurydice out to be a young man (as in high poetry, Maximin for George was a counterpart of Dante's Beatrice): Eurydice will be "the alley-cat of Hell" or she is banisht and a young man takes her place "in streams too deep for love." Spicer's wit is quick to present emotion in grimace. In "Orpheus in Hell": "Later he would remember all those dead voices / And call them Eurydice."

That vocabulary had begun for Spicer in 1946 with the second part of my poem "Heavenly City, Earthly City" in which I had projected such a confusion in the figures of Orpheus:

> Sweep, then, Orpheus, the wild music from your lyre
> as if you sang lost love, but remember
> the beauty and charm are hate's machineries,
> demonic art that catches the damnation into its disk
> and lends to hell its immortal strain.

and of Eurydice:

> Sweep, then, Orpheus, the wild love from your lips
> and when from the far room your forgiven lover
> cries out from the rejection that forgiving is,
> remember Eurydice's face because you turnd
> is turnd toward her death . . .

> remember his face as your Eurydice
> that was the woman's face in the lunar gleam of sleep.

*

In the Berkeley period 1946-1950 we dreamd—Jack Spicer, Robin Blaser and I—on the seashores of Bohemia of a

Berkeley Renaissance and projected Orphic mysteries and magics in poetry. "Among my friends love is a great sorrow" was written in 1946 before I met Jack Spicer I think. He did not originate bitterness for me, but he deepend my recognition of it. By the last months of that year, when I was in the throes of writing "Heavenly City, Earthly City," even as I was in the throes of a sexual psychodrama, Spicer was in attendance every day to witness the events or hear the aftermath of the love affair or the poem, to commiserate with the friend's suffering and to hear in rapt attention the installments of the poet's rhapsody that went so far beyond the bounds of the decorum establisht for the art. If later he was to draw upon the poem, what seems most important here is that his intensity in audience drew me on into reaches, wooing his listening, where over-riding / over-writing the actual events and relationships I raise figures of another realm of feeling in which visionary ejaculation and nightmare phantasy are confused.

In "Chinoiserie" Spicer seems to be referring directly to the impact of "Heavenly City, Earthly City" as he affirms his "share of that desiring / And that aching, slapping sound of a hundred waves." And in "An Arcadia for Dick Brown" he writes his own turbulent rhapsody in which "the pull of a Rococo wildness / aching full of fauns takes shape" and a chinaman who dances "the Pan, the Wandering Jew, the little dream the analyst forgot" and holds the key to this poetry may be the poet of that preceding poem he draws upon. I was, anyway, the first poet Spicer took to be of his order, and the obsession remains, more than a quarrel, more than a contention, a war against the figure I was for him—that's but the half of it. In the other half, I am also the one who betrayd again and again the figure I was for him. From the beginning my rhetorical mode must have been difficult for him, for he was puritan in his ethos of the poem and hostile to the "poetic," the charm or luxury of the poem. Increasingly his work would take on an apotropaic magic against the seduction of words. "Words, loves."

It was the difference between ideas of God. Had we been atheists the difference would have remaind between the ideas of God we refused. In the beginning the difference must have been one of temperament. It seems to me that we seek ideas of God because they are necessary to some picture of our own nature and world. Both of us were homosexual in orientation; but for me my homosexuality was a potentiality, a creative promise for love; for Spicer his homosexuality was a curse, a trick in the game of a God who predestined such love of man for man to damnation. Poetry was then the second brand of Cain he was condemned to carry: "My vocabulary led me to this." He was addicted to Poetry as he was to alcohol, sick unto death with it. In a letter of 1954 to Graham Macintosh, Poetry appears to be as invasive and tyrannical as the Army is for a draftee: "When we return to the chessboard there will be no more marching and making beds for you, no more losing and finding of poetry for me, we will be human beings again moving our selves across a board that has definite limits and allows for laughter." But in the 1946 poem "The Chess Game," the board is hostile to us as human beings.

*

So in his twenty-first year, Spicer sees projected—"in the cards"—the fortunes and misfortunes of a dual curse in "The Bridge Game" and "The Chess Game," as if he were reading his own palm, but significantly it is not given in the palm but in the trap of playing in the riggd game. In "The Bridge Game" the rebus of twenty years to come—he will die in his forty-first year—is given. Is it this that is his "vocabulary"? The poem declares the issue to be given in Hart Crane's tragic life and in his poem *The Bridge*: in his doomed search for homosexual love and in his adherence to the poetic quest in which his personal life and his American vision will be brought into one language. "The Bridge / Two Hearts" I read to mean here the game in which the heart devoted to love and the heart devoted to poetry are bridged to be broken (as in "An Apocalypse for Two Voices" later "the aching chord is broken"). "Everything echoes" is from the first the condition of poetry for Jack Spicer. The first words announce themselves as they fall as members of a fateful vocabulary he must follow through to the end. Not only the words one writes but the words one reads that "get to" one. Hart Crane's vocabulary as Spicer reads it to be primary becomes his own where he will in his own art echo back now plaintively, now derisively to the resounding sea—the sea of Duncan's "Heavenly City, Earthly City" rememberd, yes, but back of that the sea of Crane's "Voyages." "Two hearts," but the bid calls attention to the magic of a doubling: in writing "Crane of Hearts" is Spicer catching "Knave of Hearts," some hint of Crane's disorderd sexual adventuring.

That bid is followd by three spades and Dashiell Hammett of *The Maltese Falcon* ("The Bird") leads to a bid of two spades, "The Sam" and the "Queen." The Bird too as it becomes an eternal member of the cast of this poetry to be will double and redouble. Is it already, as it will strikingly be in "The Song of the Bird in the Loins," in the "gamecock" of "Five Words for Joe Dunn," in "A poem to the reader of the poem," or the Holy Ghost in "Song for Bird and Myself," the phallus as angel? The fraud of the bird in Hammett's mystery story is bitter then in reference. Sam Spade like Hart Crane is a prototype of the poet, but now not the victim but the hard-hearted detective who answers Brigid O'Shaughnessy when she challenges him that he knows if he loves her or not:

> "I don't. It's easy enough to be nuts about you. [This thematic stand will be taken by Spicer again and again in his life and his work and in the voice of Sam Spade] But I

don't know what that amounts to. Does anybody ever? But suppose I do? What of it? Maybe next month I won't. I've been through it before—when it lasted that long. Then what? Then I'll think I played the sap. I won't play the sap for you."

In "Some Notes on Whitman for Allen Joyce" this handing over of Whitman not to be taken in by the promise of love is the Sam Spade voice of the poet. "At least we both know how shitty the world is," he addresses Allen Ginsberg in the last poem of *Book of Magazine Verse.* "You wearing a beard as a mask to disguise it. I wearing my tired smile. I don't see how you do it." In a lasting sense Spicer does not reject life, he simply refuses to be taken in by it. He turns it over to the judgment that falls on it—predestined—as he turns himself over to judgment.

Brigid in *The Maltese Falcon* is, any way, the Queen of Spades, the Black Maria, Bad Luck: *pique dame* in french which even as I may over-reach Spicer's intended meaning is all the more telling a reading, for "pique" doubles in English as "offense taken by one slighted or disdaind, a fit of resentment" which is a pervasive mode in Spicer's feeling.

"Pass, Pass, Pass" The bird, the Maltese Falcon, passes for real. In the early years 1946-1948 Spicer was not sure whether or not he was passing sexually. A poem from that period reads "My chastities express the hermit's act / To go and bar the door." He might yet pass. Yet not escape, for the lot in this game is built in in the rules. As the cards are revealed to be Tarot, this bridge proves to be the casting, the laying on, of a fortune. "Madam Alice" will recall "Madam Sosostris" from *The Waste Land,* but now as "Alice, Alice, Miserere" the cry goes up, we realize it is Alice of those "Adventures Under Ground," and the King of Hearts, the Queen of Spades, may be Hades and Persephone, even as the Bi-cycle Playing Cards are the host of the dead:

"Now for the evidence," said the King, "and then the sentence."

"No!" said the Queen, "first the sentence, and then the evidence!"

"Nonsense!" cried Alice, so loudly that everyone jumped, "the idea of having the sentence first!"

But, just so, in this poem predicting the poetry to come it has yet to come to, it is the sentence that comes first. On the evidence of the sentence we begin to read. It is the world of Calvin's God and of Predestination that is back of this nightmare.

*

In the Pleasure Dome of Kublai Khan, in the realm of the poem, the cards as they fall in the game are "fortunes told by Madam Alice."

The conjunctions of Hermes Trismegistus, Marco Polo, and Kublai's Palace have their origins, I would venture, in John Livingston Lowes' *Road to Xanadu,* and—is it an accidental strike?—when I turn to where Hermes Trismegistus occurs in that text I find it lies in the chapter "The Bird and the Demon" on "Wingy Mysteries":

> And with the new wonders of the air which science was disclosing merged the immemorial beliefs in its invisible inhabitants, whether vouched for by Iamblichus, or Hermes Trismegistus, or Captain Cook.

What I do know is that Lowes' book in 1946 was already a key work for Spicer, where he had surely found beautifully researcht and glowingly projected the idea of a ground of lore, an intricate network of associations and informing minds beyond the poet's at work in the poem: it suggested more than sources upon which the poet drew in his inspiration; it suggested "invisible inhabitants" coming in to the poem like spirits to a medium's table. Madam Alice as she lays out the cards, like Madame Sosostris in Eliot's *Waste Land,* is not only the reader of fortunes, so that we see the poem itself as a casting of fortunes, but she is a medium reading what the spirits tell her is in the cards. In the text she reads another text, so that we see the poem also as a medium of messages. What John Livingston Lowes taught us was that no poem was an isolated or insulated product but drew upon and led in return to all that the poet or the reader of the poem had known, even what he but subconsciously rememberd, what he knew not he knew, from the world of Mind and Imagination at work in all he had experienced:

> Nobody who knows the period can dream of isolating its poetry from the ferment of its thought or of detaching Samuel Taylor Coleridge from that ferment. And when Wordsworth suggested his 'spectral persecution,' all this accumulated lore, held in solution in Coleridge's brain was precipitated in the strange vengeance which overtook in haunted seas the slayer of a solitary albatross. What the fortunate bird acquired, in fact, along with immortality, was the efficient, if belated, championship of a fully accredited Neoplatonic daemon.

As the reader of the "Books" of Spicer will be aware, Spicer was to come to a doctrine of poetry as dictation, as "spectral persecution." For a moment in "The Bridge Game" one might have passed, but Buddha's Wheel turns round into "Rod and Creel," the Father's punishing rod and the Son's fishing net. Once the wedding guest is caught by the Ancient Mariner, he will not get past. The net of the poem takes over and leads into a spell binding lives to lives—into a community of the poem. This compounding of texts belonging to the poem: *The Bridge, The Maltese Falcon, The Road to Xanadu,* "The Pleasure Dome of Kublai Khan," *Alice in Wonderland,* and, with the Ace of Cups revealed as the Holy Grail, the Grail legends, but also the lore in which Tarot and Grail legends are confused, proposes the mode Lowes found in Coleridge's imagination, of a host of energies "at work behind these fabrics of its weaving."

The movement from the Tarot cards, which Spicer knew at work in the poetry of Yeats and Eliot, to the "Courtesy Bicycle Playing Cards," from fortune or occult text (as the Tarot was also the Book of Thoth) to "Playing" Cards is a movement toward greater terror: once we are "playing," we have entered the trap itself. So too in the movement from Crane's *The Bridge* with its idealizing stand heroic to the "hard-boiled" realism of Hammett's novel. The Queen of Spades trumps the King of Hearts: when Brigid calls upon Sam Spade's heart he turns her over to the Black Maria. But it remains, the sinister woman trumps the man: can Bicycle Playing Cards mean not only the two Wheels—the Tarot rota, and Buddha's—but also bring to mind bi-sexual, the two sexes turning upon each other. "Bi-" as the fortune goes. The Hanged Man on the Wheel of sexuality. The omens of this poem forecast long shadows.

Does the "Miserere" of "The Bridge Game" go back to Psalm 51 with its prayer for mercy and its confession of rebellious spirit against the Father? back to Spicer's pursuit of Christian doctrine that so continues in his later work? We may rightly hear among these voices informing the word "Miserere" the confession: "My rebellious acts that face me I know too well, and my sin is ever before me" and the plea "in your kindness, in your immense compassion delete my rebellious acts." For the homosexual, whose very making love is bound with a desire for the Father's love, even as it is bound with the love of man for man, that if it be sexual is abominated by Jahweh, there can be no evidence of His kindness, of His compassion. The Bird here is the bird of *The Maltese Falcon,* and Brigid pleads in vain with Spade: "If the bird had been real, would you have handed me over?" Unremittingly the God of Judgment in Spicer predestines without kindness or compassion. The Game is designd to defeat kindness. In "The Chess Game" the Lord's Prayer appears in a sinister cast: "And forgive us our love as we forgive thy hatred."

*

Among my mementos of Jack Spicer is an early gift from him, his Junior Department Promotion Certificate to the Intermediate Department of the Wilshire Presbyterian Sunday School, dated June 14, 1936. In Robin Blaser's cautionary note regarding the depth of Spicer's Calvinist background, he writes: "His mother tells me that during his first college year, 1944, at the University of Redlands, he joined a Baptist or Methodist group." The God who appears in Spicer's poetry is that Creator—the Designer of the Game and of the Rules and of our Winning or Losing—who has projected upon Man the predestination of a Hell along with the agony of a sexual compulsion, a poetic compulsion, an alcoholic compulsion, a gaming compulsion, a psychodramatic compulsion that leads him deep into the defeat rooted in his given nature. Spicer, strikingly, in a period when Man's biological and cultural origins have been an important poetic research, is not a poet of origins. The Fall, even in its ecological guise, is not a leading theme with him. It is the Cheat, the Trap, designd from the beginning as the condition of the world and of our being that goads him. But back of the predominant theme, from the earliest poems to the last, of Love itself's being predestined to defeat, the Father's hatred is unremitting, and the poet, as son of his father, is eaten at the core with an abhorrence of life's conditions. Blaser is more than right that Spicer by 1946 was no longer a Calvinist. But what made for his seeking out Presbyterian schooling? There must have been first of all, I think, the search for a Jesus: the Jesus we find in Spicer's "Mr. J. Josephson, on a Friday Afternoon" who says "Reject reflected light," seeing the light's broken reflection in the glass, and "gave the world his throat to break / And made the glass opaque and real with blood"; or the Jesus we find in "The Inheritance—Palm Sunday" "a precious scarecrow, bound and crucified," Man's victim; or the Eros of "Five Words for Joe Dunn" "Who will cling to you every birthnight / bringing your heart substance" so that "whomever you touch will love you, / will feel the cling of His touch upon you / like sunlight scattered over an ancient mirror." There is a special poignancy for the homosexual lover both in his being just in his love crucified by the scorn, the disgust, and the laws of the Judaeo-Christian society he belongs to and also in his finding his ultimate beloved in this Bridegroom. In the late 1950s when I was reading the theosophical works of Jacob Boehme, Spicer urged me, Don't neglect the most important, *The Way to Christ.* And in his late work, in the set of "Four Poems for *Ramparts*" in *Book of Magazine Verse,* his allegiance is reaffirmed:

> And yet it's there. Accepting divinity as Jesus accepted humanness. Grudgingly, without passion, but the most important point to see in the world.

Here the voice passes from the mode of poetry into credo.

By 1945-46 when he came up from Redlands to the University at Berkeley, he was seeking in Buddhist readings and in universalizing and rationalizing philosophies for a belief that would supplant the religion in which he had known the misery of his soul as it confronted what it could not but see as the impossibility and prohibition of the love it needed. Robin Blaser tells us that when he first knew him, Spicer was expounding the universe of Leibnitz with its monads. Spicer in the Summer of 1946 when I met him sounded me out with the doctrines of Buddhism in which heavens and hells were but part of the fabric of illusions the mind projected. But he also asked about what I knew of the Albigensians and back of them about gnostic doctrines of the Hellenistic world, in which the Creator of this World, the Father of the Old Testament, was revealed to be Ignorant of Truth or the very Enemy of Truth, and we were his creatures only as we had been enslaved or drawn down from our true heritage. In "An Answer to a Jew" he writes:

> When asked if I am an enemy of your people,
> I would reply that I am of a somewhat older people:
> The Gay, who are neither Jew nor Goyim,
> Who were cut down in your Lord God Jehovah's first
>   pogrom
> Out at Sodom.

Both God and Man are to blame: "None of the nations ever protested about it" he adds. But the issue is deeper going than the matter of Sodom, for in the very order of the Creation, God's vengeful nature, his hatred, is felt.

In "Chess Game," the companion poem to "Bridge Game," the hopelessness of the cry "Miserere" in "Bridge Game," becomes clear. Here the universe appears where "the king is dead and the queen is mad" and Alice is locked in a dementia. "Yes, we are curved now and all the arcs / Are round with envy. / We move counterclockwise toward another Wonderland"—it is a vision of a creation that is a game where terrible angels move men like pawns toward absolute zero. Bishops, knights, and rooks, look down "on the brave little pawns / that march in solemn column toward the curve / That leads below the chessboard." "Where are the players?" the poet asks. "Perhaps they pray"; then there follows a Hell's version of the Lord's prayer. "Give us this day our daily doubt / And forgive us our love as we forgive thy hatred." It is strange indeed to come from this diabolical chess game seen so in 1946 to the chessboard of the letter to Macintosh in 1954 where the pattern is made to fit human beings. Yet it is

of the essential nature of Spicer's poetics that they co-exist:
the board where men are moved by God like pawns and the
other where "we will be human beings again moving our selves
across a board that has definite limits and allows for laughter."
Robin Blaser in his "The Practice of Outside" remembers him
"full of laughter," saying "We [Blaser, Spicer and I] were the
three immortals," for some moment standing in the Taoist
world of Tu Fu. I can only see deeper as I read in his work, no
laughter, unless it be mocking, a resolve that holds to the pro-
mise of Jesus but, even as the travesty of "as we forgive thy
hatred" sounds, will not give up the curse for it so needs the
accusation against Creation itself. In this he comes close to
Baudelaire and close indeed to Artaud. Jehovah is the other
person of Jesus.

In "Four Poems for *Ramparts*" the sentence "God is pal-
pably untrue" might be read at first take to mean that the
proposition of God is false; but the statement remains that
God is Himself untrue, as a lover is untrue. He is untrue to us
who are His creatures as a poet is untrue to his poems, untrue
in love. Then there follows what I can barely keep at the level
of belonging to the poem but it breaches that understanding
and sounds to be a confession of a rueful faith:

But Jesus dies and comes back again with holes in his hands.
    Like the weather,
And is, I hope, to be reached, and is something to pray to
And is the Son of God.

In the fourth poem of that set—"(in a dark forest be-
tween grace and hatred)" there is the confession of a need not
only for grace "Like almost, without grace, a computer cen-
ter," but also for hatred:

              Without his hatred
    A barren world.

In this later poetry, the bridge game and the chess game of the early poems become "Baseball or the name game" and the Calvinist God, or the Gnostic Lord of This World, the Demiurge, Spicer proposes now "is a big white baseball that has nothing to do but go in a curve or a straight line." If it is a conceit, it is as serious as John Donne's propositions leading as it does to the sudden revelation of a needed depth of feeling:

Off seasons
I often thought of praying to him but could not stand the
thought of that big, white, round, omnipotent bastard.

If "a curve or a straight line" might stand in a sexual level of meaning, in "the little dream that the analyst forgot," for *bent* and *straight* sexual orientation, remembering the "curve" —the curve thrown—in "Chess Game," the "him" of the passage at hand may be read anew to mean the omnipotent aroused penis in erection. At every level the suffering protest against compulsion becomes itself in a doublebind compulsive.

Yet he's there. As the game follows rules he makes them.
I know.
I was not the only one who felt these things.

*

It is throughout the authenticity of feeling that informs Spicer's poetry: the need, the mistrust, the spite, the longing, the tenderness, the playful glee, the cunning manipulation, the profound underlying depressions—whatever they are untrue to, are true to feeling. What he sought in Calvinist and gnostic theologies was an ideogram in which God's betrayal and Man's love would never change but co-exist. And in the declarations of love, the pathos of Spicer's love feeling and the chagrin, the poignancy of his remaining a love poet in the midst of what appears to be overwhelming evidence of hatred increases.

"To pierce the darkness you need a clock that tells good time," he writes in *Book of Magazine Verse:*

Something in the morning to hold on to
As one gets craftier in poetry one sees the obvious messages
(cocks for clocks) but one forgets the love that gave them
Time.

*

"Your play," our Fate says. Meeting with his fellows of the bridge game was as important for Jack Spicer as meeting with his fellows of the poetry game at Gino and Carlos or meeting with his fellow watchers of the baseball game. "North, the partner vulnerable—West, the opponent vulnerable—East, the opponent vulnerable—South, the dealer vulnerable," the table reads. And we must play the hand out.

In the bi-cycle of that word "play," the child long ago knew how playing that he was Hart Crane or Sam Spade or Alice led into his losing himself in his play—rapt, seized: to pretend as to imagine was to be transfixt, transformd. If the "Arcadia" for Dick Brown is made-up, "intentioned," a "chinoiserie," Spicer writes, it is no sooner proposed so that it is immediately "real," and Dick Brown, the actual Dick Brown, is revealed to be Nijinsky, the faun Nijinsky "playd," Beauty's very self, more true than real. What the poem creates in actual life at the time overtook Spicer himself and he was in love with Dick Brown—the poem created it in him—or is it the other way round? the poem revealed to him what otherwise he would not know he felt so? In the order of this play, Spicer's calling up of this "aching" Rococo Dresden landscape, all artifice—first cousin of Yeats' Symbolist Byzantine "gong-tormented sea"—once Dick Brown is seen to be the faun, "startling, young, streaming with beauty," the evocation itself "breaks like dawn," revealing itself to be the poet's being in love, a falling-in-love real beyond the bounds in this pretended world.

The poem in this early period was conceived as an entertainment, a serious amusement. The listener is, even as the poet is, drawn in once the play begins, distracted, bemused, and the world turns out to be funny. Not funny ha ha, but the other sense of humor, of darker humors: funny strange. Estranged. "There is more of Orpheus in Sophie Tucker than in R. P. Blackmur," Spicer says in the 1949 Symposium. Poetry was to be a vaudeville act. Vachel Lindsay, Spicer proposes as the model. The performing voice of "The Congo" and "The Chinese Nightingale" is back of Spicer's proposition. When we remember what contempt Pound had for Harriet Monroe's prize awarded to "The Chinese Nightingale" we may appreciate something of the declaration of independence in Spicer's stand.

It is this insistence upon the primary, the primitive magic reality taken in a staged magic, the deadly play-earnest working in the mask behind the face, that is Spicer's creative forte —more significantly, that is his creative task. And the act is to be American and popular. "One needs no Virgil, but an Alice, a Dorothy, a Washington horsecar conductor, to lead one," he writes in "Some Notes on Whitman for Allen Joyce": "Calamus is like Oz." This is a poetry that has common roots, or a common Road to Oz, with much of contemporary science fiction, yet it exceeds the common sense of being "fantasy," for his phantasies are taken to be not escapes from reality but descents into reality.

Spicer is not only the *miglior fabbro* of this fiction, but also creature through and through of the auto-fabrication, for the very making-believe is reveald at every stage to be not "his" but his Creator's. If Nijinsky dancing the faun presents the Beloved, the lover Spicer has his likeness presented in Nijinsky's Petrushka. The Joker in the deck of Bicycle Playing Cards is wild, somehow funny-not-funny. We don't laugh. The heart for Spicer in these poems is Hart Crane, is resisting, besieged, a dead weight—"the blood's weight under the heart's alleys pressing," falling, jagged and half-awake, twisting,

> Heart so monstrous naked that the world recoils,
> Shakes like a ladder,
> Spits like a cat.

Spicer is a master of humors, but he is never "light"-hearted. I see him as playful always, but it is the play of the moth-soul's wings caught in the meshes of the spider the soul somehow also is in its art: "Arachne . . . twisted deep like thread upon a spoiled / sewing machine" portrays the poet who is caught in the "Rags, bottles, and old beauty, bones." There is no facility, nothing facile, about Spicer's amazing and cunning wit, about his feints and strategies—for they are struggles in earnest.

Sing from the heart! Sophie Tucker's song is belted out from the heart. Love songs, blues songs. "Spook singer, hold your tongue," Spicer writes in "A Postscript to the Berkeley Renaissance"—he is funny then like a spook at Hallowe'en, a ghost dancer at the door of the heart to trick or treat.

"I sing a newer song no ghost-bird sings," he tells us: "My tongue is sharpened on the iron's edge."

ROBERT DUNCAN
San Francisco, June 1980

EDITOR'S NOTE

Jack Spicer I first met in 1948, not long after I'd separated myself from the Navy and settled in Berkeley, where we were fellow graduate students. From the first he struck me as being the most vividly original gay man I'd ever encountered anywhere. We became friends at once, and when he realized that I was attempting to write poetry too, began to give me copies of his poems and to tutor me in the fine art of writing verse. We met frequently to talk about poems and he was consistently very positive and supportive in his criticism. Those years were the heyday of the Berkeley Renaissance, and Jack was of course very active on the scene. He took me around to readings; most notably, he introduced me to Robert Duncan when we attended the informal Pound Seminar Robert was conducting weekly in his home.

In early 1950 I left Berkeley to work in publishing in New York, and Jack, who had been teaching in Minneapolis, paid me a visit during the 1951 Christmas holidays. I can still remember his reading "We find the body difficult to speak" to me in a midtown Manhattan coffeeshop one chilly afternoon. I thought at the time: this is utterly unlike any poetry being written by eastern poets and no editor I know of would even consider publishing it. Such was the dismal situation of poetry in that period.

Inevitably the question of a book came up. Jack continued to send me poems and revisions of poems with that idea more and more firmly in mind. Then when he came to New York, en route from Boston to Berkeley in November of 1956, I typed up all the MSS I had received and we spent a day together going over the poems and entering the latest revisions. The few editors of literary magazines I showed some of Jack's work were completely uninterested, as I had gloomily anticipated; but in 1957 I was able to include seven of his poems in the "San Francisco Scene" issue of *Evergreen Review.*

During that summer I nightly met Jack in North Beach bars and heard his *After Lorca* poems as he wrote them almost daily. But that seemed to be another book shaping up, and I felt we still needed a few more poems for the projected volume of his earlier writing, assuming I could interest a publisher in taking it on. When I left for New York in the fall, he promised to send me more poems; but before the end of the year he neatly got me off that hook. In an Admonition to Robin Blaser he wrote:

> "Halfway through *After Lorca* I discovered that I was writing a book instead of a series of poems and individual criticism by anyone suddenly became less important. This is true of my *Admonitions* which I will send you when complete. (I have eight of them already and there will probably be fourteen including, of course, this letter.)
>
> The trick naturally is what Duncan learned years ago and tried to teach us—not to search for the perfect poem but to let your way of writing of the moment go along its own paths, explore and retreat but never be fully realized (confined) within the boundaries of one poem. This is where we were wrong and he was right, but he complicated things for us by saying that there is no such thing as good or bad poetry. There is—but not in relation to the single poem. There is really no single poem.
>
> That is why all my stuff from the past (except the Elegies and *Troilus* [a play]) looks foul to me. The poems belong nowhere. They are one night stands filled (the best of them) with their own emotions, but pointing nowhere, as meaningless as sex in a Turkish bath. It was not my anger or my frustration that got in the way of my poetry but the fact that I viewed each anger and each frustration

as unique—something to be converted into poetry as one would exchange foreign money. I learned this from the English Department (and from the English Department of the spirit—that great quagmire that lurks at the bottom of all of us) and it ruined ten years of my poetry. Look at those other poems. Admire them if you like. They are beautiful but dumb.

Poems should echo and reecho against each other. They should create resonances. They cannot live alone any more than we can.

So don't send the box of old poetry to Don Allen. Burn it or rather open it with Don and cry over the possible books that were buried in it—the Songs Against Apollo, the Gallery of Gorgeous Gods, the Drinking Songs—all incomplete, all abortive—all incomplete, all abortive because I thought, like all abortionists, that what is not perfect had no real right to live.

Things fit together. We knew that—it is the principle of magic. Two inconsequential things can combine together to become a consequence. This is true of poems too. A poem is never by itself alone."

Then in April of 1958, when I began to lay plans for what became *The New American Poetry* anthology, I asked Jack to tell me which ten of his poems I should consider and said that, in any case, I hoped to include one "Imaginary Elegy." He replied:

"The list of poems [below] is a list of those that you have permission to choose from in selecting for the anthology. The ten checked are my ten favorites.

I would strongly prefer the 2nd Elegy rather than the 4th to be printed. The 4th can't, I think, exist by itself while the 2nd can. It (the 2nd) would be my first choice.

I give you a free hand on the whole list as you know better than I what poems by other poets it (or they) will be set against.

The After Lorcas on the list are from among those that are completely mine in the book so there would be no problem of rights. . . .

What I would really dream of is having the whole Elegies in. But I guess that's impossible, what?"

√Arcadia for Dick Brown
A Heron for Mrs. Altrocchi
Berkeley in Time of Plague
Orpheus After Eurydice
√You, Apollo
Troy Poem
√We find the Body Difficult to Speak
√Imaginary Elegies (II preferred)
Dardanella
Midnight at Bareass Beach
Sonnet for Beginning of Winter
On Reading Last Year's Love Poems
The Boy Had Never Seen an Honest Man
Orpheus in Hell
The Day 5000 Fish Died Along the Charles River
√Song for the Great Mother
Babel 3
Song for Bird and Myself
5 Words for Joe Dunn's Birthday
Notes on Walt Whitman
Frog (*After Lorca*)
Ballad of the Dead Woodcutter (*After Lorca*)
Alba (*After Lorca*)
√Aquatic Park (*After Lorca*)
Buster Keaton Rides Again (*After Lorca*)
Friday the 13th (*After Lorca*)

Afternoon (*After Lorca*)
√ Radar (*After Lorca*)
For Ebbe [*Admonitions*]
For Russ [*Admonitions*]
√ For Billy [*Admonitions*]
For Mac [*Admonitions*]
√ For Jerry [*Admonitions*]
√ Improvisation on a Sentence by Poe [*A Book of Music*]
Cantata [*A Book of Music*]
Mummer [*A Book of Music*]
Jungle Warfare [*A Book of Music*]
IInd & IIIrd & IVth Phase of the Moon
Éternnement [?]

I considered several combinations of shorter poems, but in the end we agreed on the four "Imaginary Elegies" for the anthology, and although he wrote me in September 1959— "No Yeats, no Robin. I was being cute with both."—I decided it was more politic to retain the dedication.

The present edition of Jack Spicer's uncollected poems is designed for that fortunate fellow, the general reader. It is based primarily on the manuscripts Jack gave me over a ten year period and it incorporates his revisions and title changes. His poems, as well as his letters, were written invariably in pencil on the ruled pages of grade-school composition books measuring 6¾ x 8¼ inches. His notation on one MS describes their usual condition: "Note the marks of folding in my back pocket indicating a genuine Spicer MS. Chemical investigation would also find traces of the sweat of my backside."

The order of the poems is approximately chronological. The "Imaginary Elegies" are not so easily placed. Robert Duncan recalls some elements of the first three Elegies as dating back to the late forties. When I asked Jack to give me the years of the first four for *The New American Poetry,* he wrote: "I guess you'd better call the years of composition 1950–1955 although, as you know, it was refurbished later. On acct. of 'these five years.' " The fifth and sixth Elegies were written and published in his magazine *J* in 1959; when he sent me copies he wrote: "There probably won't be more for a while. I'm working on something else." I have also included poems that were published during his lifetime as well as the few which have turned up in several posthumous publications. In several instances I have adopted more conventional spellings, but "spasmatic," which the *OED* listed in 1933 as "now rare or obsolete," has been retained.

A few notes on the poems: The late Dorothy Spicer gave me the MS of the first poem, "We bring these slender cylinders of song," in 1965 not long after Jack's death, saying it had been written some twenty years before. The second poem, "There is an inner nervousness in virgins," was reconstructed by Ariel Parkinson from memory, the original given her in 1946 having been lost, and it was published as *A Lost Poem* in 1974. The poem, "The world I felt this winter every hour," Jack decided, in 1956, was the only "non-canonical" poem in my collection. No doubt he would then have felt the same about poems he had sent Kenneth Rexroth in 1947 for a projected anthology which were not published until 1974, and then in *An Ode and Arcadia:* "Mr. J. Josephson on a Friday Afternoon," "A Lecture on Practical Aesthetics," and several untitled verses. One, beginning "Arachne was stuck with her shuttle," was later revised and titled "Ars Poetica."

"A Night in Four Parts" was so radically rewritten after Robert Duncan published it in *Berkeley Miscellany* (No. 1, 1948) that I have included both versions. "Sonnet for the Beginning of Winter" was originally called "Lyric for Gary," and "Dardenella" was incorporated, after major surgery, into

The Heads of the Town up to the Aether as "Rimbaud." I have retained the second stanza of "At a Party," which Jack deleted in 1956. "To a Certain Painter," "Epilogue in Another Language" and Rilke's "Panther" are from Graham Mackintosh's papers.

I am particularly indebted to the staff of the Bancroft Library, the University of California at Berkeley, where the MSS from Graham Mackintosh's and my collections are housed. I owe a debt of gratitude to Robert Duncan for his encouragement of this project and for assistance in dating some of the poems, and also to Paul Mariah for his helpful advice and for his pioneering "Jack Spicer Issue" of *Manroot* (1974/1975). And I am warmly grateful to John Button for getting me started again. Several poems from *The Collected Books of Jack Spicer* (1975) are included here with the kind permission of John Martin of Black Sparrow Press.

Donald Allen

ONE NIGHT STAND & OTHER POEMS

[WE BRING THESE SLENDER CYLINDERS OF SONG]

We bring these slender cylinders of song
Instead of opium or frankincense
Because the latter would not last for long
Or stay forever in your memory—hence
We bring you opium of cellulose
And frankincense inscribed in little scratches
And you can taken a big or little dose
Or have your memory in scraps and patches

And lest you might forget our joyous eyes
When age has slowed your mind and dulled your face
You'll find below a list of all the guys
Who shelled out money as their last embrace
Of fair Geneva who has made a place
Of beauty under dark and dusty skies.

[1945?]

1

[THERE IS AN INNER NERVOUSNESS IN VIRGINS]

There is an inner nervousness in virgins
And a sorrow of a kind,
The pent attention of the deaf and dumb,
The blunted sensuousness that haunts the blind.
Virginity could summon God before—
Not mine, not mine;
My chastities express the hermit's act
To go and bar the door

TO THE SEMANTICISTS

Speak softly; definition is deep
But words are deeper,
Unmoving hungry surfaces
Lying like icebergs, half-submerged
Waiting to feed, to chew the ships and spew
The half-digested sailors from their maw
Back into history.

[1946]

THE BRIDGE GAME

	The Bridge
	Two Hearts
	The Crane of Hearts, The King of Hearts
North	Spades, Spades, Spades
the	The Bird
part-	Two Spades
ner	The Sam of Spades, The Queen of Spades
Vulnerable.	Pass, Pass, Pass
	Tarot, Pharaoh, Pharaoh, Pharaoh
	Hermes Trismegistus
West	Hermes Trismegistus
the oppo-	Marco Polo, Kublai's Palace
nent vul-	FORTUNES TOLD BY MADAM ALICE
nerable.	Pass, Pass, Pass
East	Buddha's Wheel
the oppo-	Rod and Creel
nent vul-	Ace of Cups
nerable	Holy Grail
South, the dealer	Bicycle, Bicycle, Bicycle, Bi—
vulnerable	The Hanged Man.
	Alice, Alice, Miserere
	Miserere, Alice, Alice.
	The King of Hearts
	The Queen of Spades
	Courtesy Bicycle
	Courtesy Bicycle
	Courtesy Bicycle Playing Cards.

THE CHESS GAME

If cylinders ran wild and begat parallelograms
If odd spheres ran their cold noses against the universe
Who then could say where the men could move?
Bishops advancing out of space and time.
Knights cavalierly non-Euclidean.
Rooks flying in black formation faster than the speed of light.
These would look down on the brave little pawns
That march in solemn column toward the curve
That leads below the chessboard.
The king is dead and the queen is mad.
Where's Alice?
Alice should indeed be there
Imprisoned in her four-dimensional looking glass
Dimensional, dementia
Yes, we are curved now and all the arcs
Are round with envy.
We move counterclockwise toward another Wonderland.
The table upon which we play is cold
Shape-solid but with rapid, rapid
Approach to absolute zero.
Where are the players?
Do they not laugh at the antics of their men?
Perhaps they pray:
"Our father, which art in curved and thick space,
Blasphemous is thy name."
White moves.
"Thy chaos come, thy whim be done.
In time as it is in space."

Black moves.
"Give us this day our daily doubt
And forgive us our love as we forgive thy hatred."
White moves.
"And lead us not, but deliver, deliver, deliver
Amen."
No one moves

A NEW TESTAMENT

Old Jesus made a will before he died
And got as witnesses an honest mob
Of good and hungry men. "I'm satisfied
To die," he said, "for dying is my job.
I don't mind doing it to save you guys
From having to endure a second hell.
This one is bad enough, but it's your size.
It fits you, though it blisters, pretty well.
So I won't take you with me when I start
Though I can promise you you'll not be damned.
But when I take my flesh off and depart
For Godhead, I'd be sorry if I'd lammed
And left you fellows stranded, so to speak,
With nothing but a promise of rebirth.
So, this is legal: To the poor and meek
I, Jesus, of sound mind, bequeath the earth.

[1946]

[AFTER THE OCEAN, SHATTERING WITH EQUINOX]

After the ocean, shattering with equinox
Has cast the last of creatures on its shore
After the final tidal wave has turned
And churned remaining rock to sandy vestiges
Ebbing, it leaves its tide pools in our skulls
Amorphous and amphibious, we gasp
And grasp the call and rasp of all recall,
The fishly odor when a mermaid dies.

CHINOISERIE

Sea lions bark, betray the rocks,
Define the jagged edges of this night;
Everything echoes.
Contorted conch shells strew this shore—
My share of that desiring
And that aching, slapping sound of a hundred waves.

AN ARCADIA FOR DICK BROWN

The limitless and stretching mountains of the damned
Surround Arcadia; they are the hells that rise above the
    ground
Of this poetic paradise; these hills of paraffin are thick;
Their wax is roused to catch the rising dawn.
The scenery is fathomless and deep
As any fragrant ocean caught in sleep.

Terrestrial paradise is isolate.
Chameleons crawl like pilgrims down the hills
But never reach this pit of paradise; the pink
Of salamanders thrashing to the brink, thrashing
Like someone's fingers, clutching and convulsive,
But they stop; reclimb that waxen mountain to the top.

Arcadia is isolate, I said.
Intentioned wildness of a dead December forest
Punctuates the pasturings; the pull of a Rococo wildness
Aching full of fauns takes shape; the shepherdry of sleep,
The dreaming Edenward, the feverings,
Real shepherds with imaginary sheep.

Paradise crawl: the salamanders dance
Upon their greasy mountains; all the damned
Perform their daily office, climb and slide
Within the paraffin; with every licking lip
They curse the Proserpinish spring; they stress
To make a leaping—rape and rescue it.

A chinaman much older than the world
Sits quietly among the flocks; his eyes
Are landscape breaking skies; he dances too
The Pan, the Wandering Jew, the little dream the
    analyst forgot,
All these and all Rococo menacings, the key
To this Arcadian chinoiserie.

He tells me fauns are lovely. I have found a faun
Whose beauty is as sudden as the ancestral ache
Of Adam. "Take my sheep," I want to tell him, "take
    my sheep.
Make sacrifice of all their rising blood
To wake him. Let my herd be gone
And murdered for this loveless, sleepy faun."

The Chinaman says no. He says no and one eye closes;
Breaks the Dresden landscape closing; breaks the heart
In closing. He says, "Dawn must follow twilight."
He says no. (The salamander twilight dances in the wind.)
He says, "Blood must come from apples." (Eden weeps.)
"You are the killer that your brother keeps.

"You are the Adam of this spring, the Cain
Who asks return for sacrifice. You are the Eve
Who pared the bloody apple to the core
And ate the body of her youngest son.
You are the Lucifer that fell
Into this dark, bucolic hell."

The Chinaman has closed his other eye; the mountains melt.
I see my faun arrived before me like an offering.
He breaks like dawn; asleep, he breaks like dawn.
I shake him. Rising like the sun he wakens
Startling, young, streaming with beauty, tossed
Upon the fragile paradise we lost, he breaks like dawn.

Nijinski swelled like this upon the world; he showed
The plumage of a rose, a petaled faun; the clothes
Of each occasion, every beauty, burst and burned.
He learned that beauty is a sorrow. Leda's dead.
Her egg is addled madness, serpent fruit—
And he's the broken shell, divine and mute.

Now shall I tell my faun that beauty is a sorrow?
Tell my faun that rising flesh is sorrow? Tell my faun
Of Icarus and of the waxen wings dawn melted?
Salamanders sing their oily hymns to Satan from the hills.
I let him hear their singing. I am Cain,
My brother's lover and his fatal pain.

We rise and all the shapes of hell crowd out to greet us.
The enormous blood falls through the veins of landscape
Far below. We go as upward as the dawn. The dawning heat,
The fire in my faun, grows like a comet, falls—
And I have dropped my sacrificial lamb
Among the waxy pastures of the damned.

Dear God, real Shepherd, curse the setting sun
Curse all the things in nature that must fall.
Curse those who know they fall, and those who weep.
Curse sheep and curse the wolves that eat the sheep.
Curse those who taste the shreds of beauty bare
And leave the carcass for the world to eat.

9

AN APOCALYPSE FOR THREE VOICES

Lactantius writing on the Apocalypse says:
"Qui autem ab inferis suscitabantur ii praeerunt
viventibus velut judices—*They, moreover, shall
be raised from the depths that they shall stand
above the living as judges.*"

I dreamt the ocean died, gave up its dead.
The last spasmatic tides, the final waves
Were crowded with escaping ghosts; the tides
Were choked and strangled with the weight of flesh
And falling bone. And soon the homeward floating ceased.
The dead awoke. Once they had mouths and said,
"When all we dead awaken," they awoke.
When all we dead—

        (but I have talked to the king of the rats
       and I have walked with the king of
          the rats
       and I have bowed to the king of the rats
       and the king of the rats has said to me—

When all we dead—

        (but I have talked to the king of the swans
       and I have walked with the king of
          the swans
       and I have bowed to the king of the swans
       and the king of the swans has said to me—

Awaken.

The Sunday Chronicle presents the dream
In slightly different order; Angel-Face
Is chased through eight cartoons by Nemesis,
By Demon Richard Tracy; each disgrace
Each new escape, is hinted out and found
And Angel-Face is cornered, caught, and drowned.
He will arise in every Sunday Chronicle

Refaced, pursued, reburied in the lake
Till Tracy roots his ever drowning heart
Into the crossroads with a phallic stake.

Or say I turn the records in a great
Electric station, our reception famed
As far as May or Babylon and back again.
My great turntable is inevitable; it whirls
Around, around, a convoluting day
A night of static [?] sleeplessness; it plays
Requested favorites, universal things,
And millions listen, hear some tenor sing,
It's a long, long way
From Babylon in May
To this November.
But listen to the chorus
                              When we dead—
Those flat and tuneless voices
                              When we dead—
The aching chord is broken
                              When we dead awaken
                              We will do the singing.
                              We will do the singing.
Their flat electric voices
Fill the sky
And Angel-Face has floated from his grave
Again to die.

Angel-Face hires lawyers from the firm
Of Ratface, Swanface, and Beelzebub.
Mr. Ratface, well-known Persian lawyer, takes the case
Faces the court, asks manslaughter on Tracy,
Slander on my station,
Death on me for treason.
Judge Swanface tries the case without a word

And orders Juryman Beelzebub
To give me death. The juror says,
"I sentence you to drown three times
When we dead
              (The king of the rats has bowed to me)
When we dead
              (The king of the swans has bowed to me)
When we dead
              (The king of the world has bowed to me)
Awaken and the living die.

MR. J. JOSEPHSON, ON A FRIDAY AFTERNOON

The sun went through the broken bottles on the porch.
   He saw
The light respond to glass. He knew the whole,
Though real, was bad reflection; he returned the light,
Retraced the pattern and rebroke the pain that fell from light.
The problem wasn't what there was to be
But what there wasn't—and broken glass
Mirrored another world of breaking glass.
He squeezed the glass together. The reflections fell
From light through twisted glass, like Lucifer.
His would not fall. "Reject reflected light," he said.
He gave the world his throat to break
And made the glass opaque and real with blood.

ARS POETICA

Arachne was stuck with her shuttle;
And twisted deep like thread upon a spoiled
Sewing machine—poor girl, she's dead—and twisted there,
Bobbins for bones and they make pants and shirts
Of little bits of flesh.
And if you ask Arachne what of garmentry?
What of embroidered blood and seamstress sorcerings?
She'll answer if unraveled carefully,
"Rags, bottles, and old beauty, bones."

[1947]

13

4 A.M.

The many clanging bell peals loud.
The pulsing, driving sound
Falls groundwards, spent of tone.
Unbound.
I see,
Mind bent around the inner ear,
The long unfeelingness of things
Beyond all sound.

[AMONG THE COFFEE CUPS AND SOUP TUREENS
WALKED BEAUTY]

Among the coffee cups and soup tureens walked Beauty
Casual, but not unconscious of his power
Gathering dishes mucked with clinging macaroni
Unbearable in his spasmatic beauty
Sovereign in Simon's Restaurant and wreathed in power
The monarch of a kingdom yet unruled.

Now regal at a table in the Starlite Club sits Beauty
Casual but not unconscious of his power
Kept by a Mr. Blatz who manufactures girdles
Unbearable in his spasmatic beauty
Counting with kingly eye the subjects of his power
Who sleep with Beauty and are unappeased.

A LECTURE IN PRACTICAL AESTHETICS

Entering the room
Mr. Stevens on an early Sunday morning
Wore sailor-whites and helmet.
He had brought a couple with him and they danced like bears
He had brought a bottle with him and the vapors rose
From helmet, naked bottle, couple
Haloed him and wakened us.

But Mr. Stevens, listen, sight and sense are dull
And heavier than vapor and they cling
And weigh with meaning.
To floors and bottoms of the sea, horizon them
You are an island of our sea, Mr. Stevens, perhaps rare
Certainly covered with upgrowing vegetation.
You may consist of dancing animals. The bear,
Mr. Stevens, may be your emblem,
Rampant on a white field or panting in plurals above the
      floor and the ocean,
And you a bearish Demiurge, Mr. Stevens, licking vapor
Into the shape of your island. Fiercely insular.
Out of sense and sight, Mr. Stevens, you may unambiguously
      dance
Buoying the helmet and the couple,
The bottle and the dance itself—
But consider, Mr. Stevens, though imperceptible,
We are also alive. It is not right that you should merely
      touch us.
Besides, Mr. Stevens, any island in our sea
Needs a geographer.

A geographer, Mr. Stevens, tastes islands
Finds in this macro-cannibalism his own microcosm.
To form a conceit, Mr. Stevens, in finding you
He chews upon his flesh. Chews it, Mr. Stevens,
Like Donne down to the very bone.
An island, Mr. Stevens, should be above such discoveries,
Available but slightly mythological.
Our resulting map will be misleading.
Though it be drawn, Mr. Stevens,
With the blood and flesh of both superimposed
As ink on paper, it will be no picture, no tourist postcard
Of the best of your contours reflected on water.
It will be a map, Mr. Stevens, a county stiffened into symbols
And that's poetry too, Mr. Stevens, and I'm a geographer.

[COME WATCH THE LOVE BALLOON]

Come watch the love balloon, that great
Inflated tautology of angel wings.
(They say it floats somewhere but I have seen
Its stupid flutter like the great sea birds
Who stumble through the city in a storm.)
Its cord goes downwards, watch the dangling men
Upon its drawstrings, watch a sudden wind
Give them a shaking; tangle, change, and bind.
Each wind is fatal. Nothing knows its place.
Beneath that high-flown floater love is like a race
Between the horse and crouching rider; no one wins,
And neither stops till someone wins—or falls.

A HERON FOR MRS. ALTROCCHI

Blue-rooted heron standing in the lake
Standing in unguessed song; like me no traveler.
Taking unsinging rest, loose-winged water-bird,
And dumb with music like the lake is dumb.

I stand upon the waterfront, like him no traveler,
Pink-rooted, dangling on my flightless wings.
Aching for flight, for swan-sung voyaging,
I wait that final thrust and take my rest.

They will not hunt us with snares and with arrows.
The flesh of the water-bird is tough and is dumb.
The sound of an arrow, the sight of a hunter
Only remind us of life without wings.

Then let us die, for death alone is motion,
And death alone can make these herons fly.
Though stiff and wingless, we will cross an ocean
On throats too huge for silence when we die.

[THE DANCING APE]

The dancing ape is whirling round the beds
Of all the coupled animals; they, sleeping there
In warmth of sex, ignore his fur and fuss
And feel no terror in his gait of loneliness.
Quaint though the dancer is, his furry fists
Are locked like lightning over all their heads.
His legs are thrashing out in discontent
As if they were the lightning's strict embodiment.
But let the dancing stop, the apish face go shut in sleep,
The hands unclench, the trembling legs go loose—
And let some curious animal bend and touch that face
With nuzzling mouth, would not the storm break—
And that ape kiss?

[THE WORLD I FELT THIS WINTER]

The world I felt this winter every hour
Becomes more tense, and now I watch the spring
Suspended like a sweating thundershower
Above a land of cold imagining,
My heart resists. I feel my senses cower
As silent as a bird with wounded wing
While every body, branch, and leaf, and flower
Rumbles with hot and lovely threatening.

Come spring, come thunder, and besiege my heart,
That north whose isobars of guilt and fear
Have kept my weather and the world's apart
And made my body's winter last the year.
Send fertile showers, make my senses smart
And ripen, with the smell of lightning near.

ORPHEUS AFTER EURYDICE

Then I, a singer and hunter, fished
In streams too deep for love.
A god grew there, a god grew there,
A wet and weblike god grew there.
Mella, mella peto
In medio flumine.
His flesh is honey and his bones are made
Of brown, brown sugar and he is a god.
He is a god.
I know he is a god.
Mella, mella peto
In medio flumine.
Drink wine, I sang, drink cold red wine.
Grow liquid, spread yourself.
O bruise yourself, intoxicate yourself,
Dilute yourself.
You want to web the rivers of the world.
You want to glue the tides together with yourself.
You look so innocent—
Water wouldn't melt in your mouth.
I looked and saw him weep a honey tear.
I, Orpheus, had raised a water god
That wept a honey tear.
Mella, mella peto
In medio flumine.

ORPHEUS IN HELL

When he first brought his music into hell
He was absurdly confident. Even over the noise of the
    shapeless fires
And the jukebox groaning of the damned
Some of them would hear him. In the upper world
He had forced the stones to listen.
It wasn't quite the same. And the people he remembered
Weren't quite the same either. He began looking at faces
Wondering if all of hell were without music.
He tried an old song but pain
Was screaming on the jukebox and the bright fire
Was pelting away the faces and he heard a voice saying,
    "Orpheus!"
                    He was at the entrance again
And a little three-headed dog was barking at him.
Later he would remember all those dead voices
And call them Eurydice.

ORPHEUS' SONG TO APOLLO

You, Apollo, have yoked your horse
To the wrong sun.
You have picked the wrong flower.
Breaking a branch of impossible
Green-stemmed hyacinth
You have found thorns and postulated a rose.
Sometimes we were almost like lovers
(As the sun almost touches the earth at sunset)
But,
At touch,
The horse leapt like an ox
Into another orbit of roses, roses.
Perhaps,
If the moon were made of cold green cheese,
I could call you Diana.
Perhaps,
If a knife could peel that rosy rind,
It would find you virgin as a star.
Too hot to move.
Nevertheless,
This is almost goodbye.
You,
Fool Apollo,
Stick
Your extra roses somewhere where they'll keep.
I like your aspiration
But the sky's too deep
For fornication.

TROY POEM

We,
Occasioned by the eye,
To look
And looking down
Saw that your city was not Troy.

Oh,
Merry Greeks,
We bear our fathers on our backs
And burdened thus
We kiss your city.

Neither
At foot or eye
Do we taste
Ruined Troy
Which was our mother.

Oh,
Merry Greeks,
When you embrace us
We, bending, thus
Pray against you:

"Rise
From our absent city
Tough as smoke——
Oh,
Flesh of Hector,
Rescue us."

DIALOGUE BETWEEN INTELLECT AND PASSION

"Passion is alien to intellect
As hot black doves are alien to trees
On which they do not rest—
All are alone.
Of passion and of intellect
Suspect
Neither bird nor tree
Of vicious privacy—
Nothing is intimate.
Doves without rest
Must blackly test
Each branch with every claw they lack
And trees alone
are tough as thrones
With too much sovereignty."

"Above your branches every hot black dove
Protests his love
And gather[s] in great swarms
As darkness comes.
They wait
Until the darkness make
Them dream-birds black
As needles and as ultimate.
As you branch blanketed in royalty
Each lacking claw, bird-real,
Will find its rest
Throughout your naked branches,
Make you feel
Birds in the bed
Locking their claws against
Your privacy."

A NIGHT IN FOUR PARTS
(First Version)

For Mr. L.E., the onlie
begetter of these nightmares.

Part I: GOING TO SLEEP

Stars shake and under the old moon
The cat leaps with casual malice—
Upsetting sleep and timber without sound
Upsetting star and sleeper without sound—
Only the dead weight of the heart's motion
Falling in response.
Without sleep and under the old moon
The cat prowls into cold places—
This is no cat-heart springing without heat.
This is no moon-heart moving without heat.
Only the blood's weight under the heart's alleys
Pressing in response.

Part II: LIGHT SLEEPING

Among
The white angry light of the moon
And the flickings of cattails
It dreams and catches all;
Spawns eye, spawns mouth,
Spawns throat, spawns genitals.
Man is so monstrous naked that the world recoils,
Shrieks like a mandrake
Cries like a cat,
Disappears.

Part III: WET DREAM

Downward it plunges through the walls of flesh;
Heart falls
Through lake and cavern under sleep
Deep like an Orpheus.
A beating mandolin
Plucking the plectrum of the moon upon its strings,
It sings, it sings, it sings.
It sings, "Restore, restore, Eurydice to life.
      Oh, take the husband and return the wife."
It sings still deeper, conjures by its spell
Eurydice, the alley-cat of Hell.
      "Meow, meow, Eurydice's not dead.
      Oh, find a cross-eyed tomcat for my bed."
Too late, too late, it was too late he fell.
The sounds of singing and the sounds of Hell
Become a swarm of angry orange flies
And naked Orpheus, moon-shriveled, dies
And rises leaving lost Eurydice.
Heart flutters upward towards humanity
Jagged and half-awake.

Part IV: WAKING

It wakes and under the new sun
An old self slowly emerges.
This is no moon-self shrinking from the sun
This is no cat-self slinking from the sun—
Only the sober weight of the day's passions
Narrowing response.
Self winds heart-self like a watch, disremembers
The almost-unmechanical, the inhuman.
Chastens itself with water, dresses——

"What was that dream I had, heart-self?
Answer!"
Can't answer.

[1948]

A NIGHT IN FOUR PARTS
(*Revised Version*)

Part I: GOING TO SLEEP

> While the heart twists
> On a cold bed
> Without sleep,
> Under the hot light
> Of an angry moon
> A cat leaps.
> The cat prowls
> Into cold places,
> But the heart stays
> Where the blood is.

Part II: LIGHT SLEEPING

> Down in the world
> Where the cat prowls,
> Heart's manikin,
> His climbing doll
> Prepares for love:
> Spawns eye, spawns mouth,
> Spawns throat, spawns genitals.
> Heart is so monstrous naked that the world recoils,
> Shakes like a ladder,
> Spits like a cat,
> Disappears.

Part III: WET DREAM

Downward it plunges through the walls of flesh,
Heart falls
Through lake and cavern under sleep
Deep like an Orpheus
A beating mandolin
Plucking the plectrum of the moon upon its strings,
It sings, it sings, it sings.
It sings, "Restore, restore, Eurydice to life.
    Oh, take the husband or return the wife."
It sings still deeper, conjures by its spell
Eurydice, the alley cat of Hell.
    "Meow, meow, Eurydice's not dead.
    Oh, find a cross-eyed tomcat for my bed."
Too late, it was too late he fell.
The sounds of singing and the sounds of Hell
Become a swarm of angry orange flies
And naked Orpheus, moon-shriveled, dies
And rises leaving lost Eurydice.
His heart fallen upward towards humanity
Howling and half-awake.

Part IV: WAKING

Heart wakes
Twists like a cat on hot bricks
Beating off sunlight.
Now the heart slinks back to the blood
And the day starts.
Then the blood asks,
"Who was that lover
That thrashed you around last night?"
And the heart can't answer.

AT A PARTY

I watched the lovers falling in the dark
Like heavy autumn leaves upon a lake.
They were so very slow it almost seemed
That every color had belonged to them.
Bright shirts and bursting jeans by candlelight
Flickered and fell apart. Then it was late
The bottom of the water had been touched
Love's limit reached, and every color lost.

I waited for you on the balcony.
We trembled like two leaves caught in the sky.
You were so drunk the reeling world stood still.
I was so sober I could see stars fall.
We could not always stay suspended there.
We floated down and touched the lake together.
I noticed that your eyes had lost their color
When we had reached the bottom of the air.

LIVES OF THE PHILOSOPHERS: DIOGENES

He spilled his seed upon the marketplace
While all the Greek boys watched. Along the street
The dogs were basking in the August sun,
Scratching their fleas, and panting with the heat.
The brown-thighed boys looked on in discontent
For they had hoped another Socrates
Would pat their heads and talk, and at the end
Confirm their daily wisdom with a kiss.
"Diogenes is Socrates gone mad,"
Their voices shouted, but his sweating face
Was straining towards the sun, blind to the light
That streamed around him through the marketplace.
The boys had left him and the dogs began
To howl in cynic wonder at the heat.

[THE BOY HAD NEVER SEEN AN HONEST MAN]

The boy had never seen an honest man.
He looked among us every night he said.
He eyed each stranger like Diogenes
And took him with his lantern into bed.
He'd probe the stranger's body with that light
Search every corner of his flesh and bone
But truth was never there. He'd spend the night
Then leave him and resume his search alone.
I tried to tell him there was some mistake
That truth's a virtue only strangers lack.
But when he turned to face me with a kiss
I closed my lying heart against his lips.

DARDENELLA

They said he was nineteen. He had been kissed
So many times his face was frozen closed.
His eyes would watch the lovers walking past.
His throat would sing, and nothing else would move.

We grownups at the bar would watch him sing.
Christ, it was funny with what tired grace
He sang our blues for us. His frozen lips
Would twist and sing the blues out song by song.

Such crazy songs. I wonder what he dreams
When kissing's over and he sleeps alone.
If something sings a lullaby for him
Out of the ancient years when he was young.

ONE NIGHT STAND

Listen, you silk hearted bastard,
I said in the bar last night,
You wear those dream clothes
Like a swan out of water.
Listen, you wool-feathered bastard,
My name, just for the record, is Leda
I can remember pretending
That your red silk tie is a real heart
That your raw wool suit is real flesh
That you could float beside me with a swan's touch
Of casual satisfaction.

But not the swan's blood.

Waking tomorrow, I remember only
Somebody's feathers and his wrinkled heart
Draped loosely in my bed.

[WHEN YOUR BODY BRUSHED AGAINST ME]

When your body brushed against me I remembered
How we used to catch butterflies in our hands
Down in the garden.
We were such patient children
Following them from flower to flower
Waiting and hoping.
With our cupped hands we used to catch them
And they answered us with a soft tickle
For they never stopped flying.
In bed I remembered them and cried for
The touch of their fast wings, the impatience
Of their bright colors
I am too old for such games
But even tonight, now your body has reminded me
      of butterflies
I lie here awake, pretending.

ON READING LAST YEAR'S LOVE POEMS

The heart's a sprinting thing and hammers fast.
The word is slow and rigid in its pace.
But, if they part once, they must meet at last
As when the rabbit and the tortoise race.
Words follow heartbeats, arrogant and slow
As if they had forever in their load,
As if the race were won, as if they go
To meet a dying rabbit on the road.
Then, step by step, the words become their own.
The turtle creeps ahead to win the prize.
But, ah, the sweeter touch, the quicker boon
Is lost forever when the rabbit dies.

THE SCROLLWORK ON THE CASKET

To walk down the streets with a dead man or to hold conversation with him over coffee in a public restaurant would be hopelessly eccentric. To entertain a corpse in private, to worry him in the privacy of one's room or in the cramped and more frightening privacy of a short story is an eccentricity more easily forgivable.

A short story is narrower than a room in a cheap hotel; it is narrower than the wombs through which we descended. It does violence to any large dead man to force him within it. To fit him (even his body) into the casket of a few paragraphs, he must be twisted and contorted; his stiff arms, his extended legs must be hacked or broken. A rigor mortis operates within the memory; his image stiffens and resists in every inch. One must maim him to fit him in.

Then, when success is achieved and the sweating author has managed to get shut his casket of paragraphs, hammering on it in a perfect fury to keep the body from bursting out, what then? He has a casket, a small regular box with a corpse inside it, and he can sell it on the market where such boxes are sold—and it has been safer, it has been less eccentric and altogether more profitable than walking down the streets with a dead man ever could have been.

There are some complaints from the customers, however. These caskets all look alike. They are brown or gray or purple (almost never black), the customers complain that they don't look very much like people.

The customers are right. The outside of the casket is made up mostly of the writer, his descriptions, his feelings, his fancies, his regrets—little or nothing about the corpse on the inside. Nothing but a few spoken words. But it is those words, only them, which give the third dimension to the story, show that there is space inside the casket. For this reason whenever I read a short story I skip through the narrative paragraphs and concentrate on the dialogue. (That is the scrollwork on the casket.)

"Whenever I read a short story," Ken said, looking up from his coffee, "I skip through the narrative paragraphs and concentrate on the dialogue." He paused for a moment. "And that's the scrollwork on the casket," he added parenthetically.

It is Ken, of course, who is dead. It is his casket I hammer now. Obviously there is something hallucinatory in the hammering of caskets. Whenever I hammer a nail into the outside of the casket, I can hear someone, on the inside, also hammering a nail. That's the trouble with this burial business; it's hard to know who's on the inside and who's on the outside, whether the living bury the dead or the dead bury the living.

"The dead bury the living," Ken said. He pulled his coat tightly around his shoulders and walked a few yards ahead of me. "The dead never return to the living; it is the living that return to the dead. People search out the ghosts they find." He walked silently ahead of me for a while and then stopped. He leaned against a heavy box and looked at me with something like pity. "I think I'm going to be sick," he said.

I think I'm going to be sick.

PSYCHOANALYSIS: AN ELEGY

What are you thinking about?

I am thinking of an early summer.
I am thinking of wet hills in the rain
Pouring water. Shedding it
Down empty acres of oak and manzanita
Down to the old green brush tangled in the sun,
Greasewood, sage, and spring mustard.
Or the hot wind coming down from Santa Ana
Driving the hills crazy,
A fast wind with a bit of dust in it
Bruising everything and making the seed sweet.
Or down in the city where the peach trees
Are awkward as young horses,
And there are kites caught on the wires
Up above the street lamps,
And the storm drains are all choked with dead branches.

What are you thinking?

I think that I would like to write a poem that is slow as
      a summer
As slow getting started
As 4th of July somewhere around the middle of the second
      stanza
After a lot of unusual rain
California seems long in the summer.
I would like to write a poem as long as California
And as slow as a summer.
Do you get me, Doctor? It would have to be as slow
As the very tip of summer.
As slow as the summer seems
On a hot day drinking beer outside Riverside
Or standing in the middle of a white-hot road

Between Bakersfield and Hell
Waiting for Santa Claus.

What are you thinking now?

I'm thinking that she is very much like California.
When she is still her dress is like a roadmap. Highways
Traveling up and down her skin
Long empty highways
With the moon chasing jackrabbits across them
On hot summer nights.
I am thinking that her body could be California
And I a rich Eastern tourist
Lost somewhere between Hell and Texas
Looking at a map of a long, wet, dancing California
That I have never seen.
Send me some penny picture-postcards, lady,
Send them.
One of each breast photographed looking
Like curious national monuments,
One of your body sweeping like a three-lane highway
Twenty-seven miles from a night's lodging
In the world's oldest hotel.

What are you thinking?

I am thinking of how many times this poem
Will be repeated. How many summers
Will torture California
Until the damned maps burn
Until the mad cartographer
Falls to the ground and possesses
The sweet thick earth from which he has been hiding.

What are you thinking now?

I am thinking that a poem could go on forever.

BERKELEY IN TIME OF PLAGUE

Plague took us and the land from under us,
Rose like a boil, enclosing us within.
We waited and the blue skies writhed a while
Becoming black with death.

Plague took us and the chairs from under us,
Stepped cautiously while entering the room
(We were discussing Yeats); it paused a while
Then smiled and made us die.

Plague took us, laughed and reproportioned us,
Swelled us to dizzy, unaccustomed size.
We died prodigiously; it hurt a while
But left a certain quiet in our eyes.

THE SONG OF THE BIRD IN THE LOINS

A swallow whispers in my loins
So I can neither lie or stand
And I can never sleep again
Unless I whisper you his song:

"Deep in a well," he whispers. "Deep
As diamonds washed beneath the stone
I wait and whisper endlessly
Imprisoned in a well of flesh.

"At night he sometimes sleeps and dreams.
At night he sometimes does not hear my voice.
How can I wound you with my well of sound
If he can sleep and dream beneath its wounds?

"I whisper to you through his lips.
He is my cage, you are my source of song.
I whisper to you through a well of stone.
Listen at night and you will hear him sing:

" 'A swallow whispers in my loins
So I can neither lie or stand
And I can never sleep again
Unless I whisper you this song.' "

[WE FIND THE BODY DIFFICULT TO SPEAK]

We find the body difficult to speak,
The face too hard to hear through,
We find that eyes in kissing stammer
And that heaving groins
Babble like idiots.
Sex is an ache of mouth. The
Squeak our bodies make
When they rub mouths against each other
Trying to talk.
Like silent little children we embrace,
Aching together.
And love is emptiness of ear. As cure
We put a face against our ear
And listen to it as we would a shell,
Soothed by its roar.
We find the body difficult, and speak
Across its wall like strangers.

A POSTSCRIPT TO THE BERKELEY RENAISSANCE

What have I lost? When shall I start to sing
A loud and idiotic song that makes
The heart rise frightened into poetry
Like birds disturbed?

I was a singer once. I sang that song.
I saw the thousands of bewildered birds
Breaking their cover into poetry
Up from the heart.

What have I lost? We lived in forests then,
Naked as jaybirds in the ever-real,
Eating our toasted buns and catching flies,
And sometimes angels, with our hooting tongues.

I was a singer once. In distant trees
We made the forests ring with sacred noise
Of gods and bears and swans and sodomy,
And no one but a bird could hear our voice.

What have I lost? The trees were full of birds.
We sat there drinking at the sour wine
In gallon bottles. Shouting song
Until the hunters came.

I was a singer once, bird-ignorant.
Time with a gun said, "Stop,
Find other forests. Teach the innocent."
God got another and a third
Birdlimed in Eloquence.

What have I lost? At night my hooting tongue,
Naked of feathers and of softening years,
Sings through the mirror at me like a whippoorwill
And then I cannot sleep.

"I was a singer once," it sings.
"I sing the song that every captured tongue
Sang once when free and wants again to sing.
But I can sing no song I have not sung."

What have I lost? Spook singer, hold your tongue.
I sing a newer song no ghost-bird sings.
My tongue is sharpened on the iron's edge.
Canaries need no trees. They have their cage.

[1954]

IMAGINARY ELEGIES

for Robin Blaser

"All the philosophy a man needs is in Berkeley."
—W. B. Yeats

I

Poetry, almost blind like a camera
Is alive in sight only for a second. Click,
Snap goes the eyelid of the eye before movement
Almost as the word happens.
One would not choose to blink and go blind
After the instant. One would not choose
To see the continuous Platonic pattern of birds flying
Long after the stream of birds had dropped or had nested.
Lucky for us that there are visible things like oceans
Which are always around,
Continuous, disciplined adjuncts
To the moment of sight.
Sight
But not so sweet
As we have seen.
When I praise the sun or any bronze god derived from it
Don't think I wouldn't rather praise the very tall blond boy
Who ate all of my potato-chips at the Red Lizard.
It's just that I won't see him when I open my eyes
And I will see the sun.
Things like the sun are always there when the eyes are open
Insistent as breath.
One can only worship
These cold eternals for their support of
What is absolutely temporary.

But not so sweet.
The temporary tempts poetry
Tempts photographs, tempts eyes.
I conjure up
From photographs
The birds
The boy
The room in which I began to write this poem
All
My eye has seen or ever could have seen
I love
I love — The eyelid clicks
I see
Cold poetry
At the edge of their image.
It is as if we conjure the dead and they speak only
Through our own damned trumpets, through our damned
      medium:
"I am little Eva, a Negro princess from sunny heaven."
The voice sounds blond and tall.
"I am Aunt Minnie. Love is sweet as moonlight here
      in heaven."
The voice sounds blond and tall.
"I'm Barnacle Bill. I sank with the Titanic. I rose in
      salty heaven."
The voice sounds blond, sounds tall, sounds blond and tall.
"Goodbye from us in spiritland, from sweet Platonic
      spiritland.
You can't see us in spiritland, and we can't see at all."

II

God must have a big eye to see everything
That we have lost or forgotten. Men used to say
That all lost objects stay upon the moon
Untouched by any other eye but God's.
The moon is God's big yellow eye remembering
What we have lost or never thought. That's why
The moon looks raw and ghostly in the dark.
It is the camera shots of every instant in the world
Laid bare in terrible yellow cold.
It is the objects we never saw.
It is the dodos flying through the snow
That flew from Baffinland to Greenland's tip
And did not even see themselves.
The moon is meant for lovers. Lovers lose
Themselves in others. Do not see themselves.
The moon does. The moon does.
The moon is not a yellow camera. It perceives
What wasn't, what undoes, what will not happen.
It's not a sharp and clicking eye of glass and hood. Just old,
Slow infinite exposure of
The negative that cannot happen.
Fear God's old eye for being shot with ice
Instead of blood. Fear its inhuman mirror blankness
Luring lovers.
Fear God's moon for hexing, sticking pins
In forgotten dolls. Fear it for wolves.
For witches, magic, lunacy, for parlor tricks.

The poet builds a castle on the moon
Made of dead skin and glass. Here marvelous machines
Stamp Chinese fortune cookies full of love.
                                        Tarot cards
Make love to other Tarot cards. Here agony
Is just imagination's sister bitch.
This is the sun-tormented castle which
Reflects the sun. Da dada da.
The castle sings.
Da. I don't remember what I lost. Dada.
The song. Da. The hippogriffs were singing.
Da dada. The boy. His horns
Were wet with song. Dada.
I don't remember. Da. Forgotten.
Da. Dada. Hell. Old butterface
Who always eats her lovers

Hell somehow exists in the distance
Between the remembered and the forgotten.
Hell somehow exists in the distance
Between what happened and what never happened
Between the moon and the earth of the instant
Between the poem and God's yellow eye.
Look through the window at the real moon.
See the sky surrounded. Bruised with rays.
But look now, in this room, see the moon-children
Wolf, bear, and otter, dragon, dove.
Look now, in this room, see the moon-children
Flying, crawling, swimming, burning
Vacant with beauty.
Hear them whisper.

III

God's other eye is good and gold. So bright
The shine blinds. His eye is accurate. His eye
Observes the goodness of the light it shines
Then, pouncing like a cat, devours
Each golden trace of light
It saw and shined.
Cat feeds on mouse. God feeds on God. God's goodness is
A black and blinding cannibal with sunny teeth
That only eats itself.
Deny the light
God's golden eye is brazen. It is clanging brass
Of good intention.
It is noisy burning clanging brass.
Light is a carrion crow
Cawing and swooping. Cawing and swooping.
Then, then there is a sudden stop.
The day changes.
There is an innocent old sun quite cold in cloud.
The ache of sunshine stops.
God is gone. God is gone.
Nothing was quite as good.
It's getting late. Put on your coat.
It's getting dark. It's getting cold.
Most things happen in twilight
When the sun goes down and the moon hasn't come
And the earth dances.
Most things happen in twilight
When neither eye is open
And the earth dances.
Most things happen in twilight
When the earth dances
And God is blind as a gigantic bat.

The boys above the swimming pool receive the sun.
Their groins are pressed against the warm cement.
They look as if they dream. As if their bodies dream.
Rescue their bodies from the poisoned sun,
Shelter the dreamers. They're like lobsters now
Hot red and private as they dream.
They dream about themselves.
They dream of dreams about themselves.
They dream they dream of dreams about themselves.
Splash them with twilight like a wet bat.
Unbind the dreamers.
                                        Poet,
Be like God.

        IV
Yes, be like God. I wonder what I thought
When I wrote that. The dreamers sag a bit
As if five years had thickened on their flesh
Or on my eyes. Wake them with what?
Should I throw rocks at them
To make their naked private bodies bleed?
No. Let them sleep. This much I've learned
In these five years in what I spent and earned:
Time does not finish a poem.
The dummies in the empty funhouse watch
The tides wash in and out. The thick old moon
Shines through the rotten timbers every night.
This much is clear, they think, the men who made
Us twitch and creak and put the laughter in our throats
Are just as cold as we. The lights are out.
                                The lights are out.
You'll smell the oldest smells—
The smell of salt, of urine, and of sleep

Before you wake. This much I've learned
In these five years in what I've spent and earned:
Time does not finish a poem.
What have I gone to bed with all these years?
What have I taken crying to my bed
For love of me?
Only the shadows of the sun and moon
The dreaming groins, their creaking images.
Only myself.
                    Is there some rhetoric
To make me think that I have kept a house
While playing dolls? This much I've learned
In these five years in what I've spent and earned:
That two-eyed monster God is still above.
I saw him once when I was young and once
When I was seized with madness, or was I seized
And mad because I saw him once. He is the sun
And moon made real with eyes.
He is the photograph of everything at once. The love
That makes the blood run cold.
But he is gone. No realer than old
Poetry. This much I've learned
In these five years in what I've spent and earned:
Time does not finish a poem.
Upon the old amusement pier I watch
The creeping darkness gather in the west.
Above the giant funhouse and the ghosts
I hear the seagulls call. They're going west
Toward some great Catalina of a dream
Out where the poem ends.
                        But does it end?
The birds are still in flight. Believe the birds.

                        [1950-55]

V

Another wrong turning
Another five years. I can't see
The birds, the island, anything
But vacant shifts and twists of the tunnel
That means
Another five years I can't see.
Or were they all right turnings
The shifts of one sense of a word to another
The birds flying there inside the eaves with their
      wings dangling
Not bats, birds.
And offering up your life to summon anything is a pretty
      silly thing.
      I can't see
Where their messages get me. Another five years
Their wings
Glittering in its black ab/sense.

For the birds. Whose live-r is torn out. Whose live-r is
      torn out.
      Pro-me-thee-us. The old turning.

Where their messages get me. The shifts
Of their beaks. Their hungry beaks. But the birds are real
      not only in feeding. I think
Their wings. Glittering in the black ab/sense.
Pro-me-thee-us. Our mouths water
Like an ocean.

And so I say to you, Jim, do not become too curious about
      your poetry
let it speed into the tunnel by itself
Do not follow it, do not try to ride it

Let it go into the tunnel and out the other side and back
  to you while you do important things like loving and
  learning patience
Five years. The train with its utterly alien cargo moving on the
  black track.

  Prometheus was a guy who had his liver eaten out by
birds. A bum who rode a black train. Who was curious.
  Play it cool with Williams or paranoid with Pound but
never ride it past the tunnel or look for a conductor to ask
  questions
  Hide, and do not ask the questions,
  At the black throat of the tunnel.

Pro - me - thee - us
Pro - me - thee - us
Five years
The song singing from its black throat.

  VI
Dignity
Dig - nity
The extra syllables are unimportant. Have no dignity, no
  meaning on this world.
Nity. Hear those syllables and dig is an obvious pun for
  digging graves or whatever that gravedigger is doing
  at the moment.
The extra syllables are unimportant. I should have loved
  him yesterday
The boy whistles
Dig -
      nity
Or like that little window in Alice which she can't go through
  because she's 27 feet tall because she ate a bottle called
  Drink Me

Po - etery. Po - eatery. The eaxtra slyllables is unimportant.
    because the poem said Drink Me. I'll find a substitute
For all your long -
Ing.
And that little door with all those wheels in it
Be -
    leave in it
Like God.

                                                    [1959]

WATCHING A TV BOXING MATCH IN OCTOBER

The boxers show an equilibrium
Unmatched this autumn. In the air outside
Winds swirl around the big October moon
While men and boxers seek a place to hide.
Within the focus of a crowded screen
The boxers face each other. They pretend
That man can counterpunch real enemies.
They hit each other til the very end.
One wins and they embrace there while the wind
Grows louder and the screen begins to fade.
Then all the men and boxers bind their wounds
Behind an empty screen, and are afraid.

MINNEAPOLIS: INDIAN SUMMER

What did the Indians do
In a hot Indian October?
Did the same things, I suppose,
Saw the birds flying,
Gathered the last corn.
The same things . . .
Saw the birds flying,
Followed their muddy river
Looking the last time
For a warm face
To kiss in the winter.
The same things . . .
Their muddy river still muddy.
The woods choked with red leaves . . .
Under a sun bright like a broken promise
Watched the birds flying.
And dirty October
Moved like their river
With a heat that frightened the birds away.

[1951?]

ALL HALLOWS EVE

Bring on the pumpkin colored wine.
The ghosts of autumn ask our pardon—
The withered flowers in the garden,
The fruit that frosted on the vine.

Each fickle life that testified
The summer's quick magnificence
Now masks its own significance
And plays the spook to salve our pride.

They wear bright costumes of the dead
And posture in a clownish way.
The lover that we loved last May
Now wears a gaping pumpkin head.

Our flowers and our lovers all
Implore us from the icy streets
And every painted spook repeats
The gestures of his burial.

Come drink the wine and watch them play
For there is nothing to be said.
No exorcist can drive away
The childish faces of the dead.

CHRISTMAS EVE: 1952

In our good house we'll light a Christmas fire
And watch each other's faces in the flame.
The very angels will be stricken dumb
To see two lovers using such a mirror.
And when the shepherds knock upon the door
Demanding news of God's nativity,
We'll let them kneel behind our Christmas tree
And watch the fire glitter on its star.

TRAIN SONG FOR GARY

The trains move quietly upon
The tracks outside like animals
I hear them every night.

And sometimes I can almost see
Their glittering unhurried eyes
Move out of sight.

I think that on the day I leave
This town of quiet houses they
Will sound their horns.

I think that then that burning herd
Will turn and follow me towards you
Like unicorns.

SONNET FOR THE BEGINNING OF WINTER

A kind of numbness fills your heart and mine,
A gap where things and people once had been.
We fell unloved, like frozen fields of snow
Upon which not a track has broken through.
The robin and the thrush have taken wing.
The sparrow stays. He sings a dismal song
And eats the seed uncovered in the snow.
An ugly bird, call him the heart's agony.

His songs of disbelief will fill our hearts
As long as winter lasts, as long as we
Are distant partners of this agony
Too far apart to keep each other warm.
So let our hearts lie dead like fields of snow
Unloved, untouched until the distant spring
Grows closer and the gentle birds return
And fill the empty air, and sing.

THE INHERITANCE — PALM SUNDAY

He rode into the vineyards on an ass
Reclaiming all the vintage of the land.
The stubborn husbandmen who watched him pass
Cursed silently and spat. He would demand
The crops his father left them to possess,
The dusty grapes, the barren ancient sheaves
Of bitter wheat, the fig trees powerless
To harvest anything but wood and leaves.
His words were soft, but those that kept the field
Struck him with calloused hands, unpacified,
And there was added to that season's yield
A precious scarecrow, bound and crucified.

[1954]

MIDNIGHT AT BAREASS BEACH

The surfaces are moving with the sound
Black water makes. As far as I can see
Out from each clinging wave, eternity
Moves back and forth, as black as nothing else.
Cold to the touch, it oozes at my feet
And lies protesting like a dog, then sighs
And slaps again. But what remains out there
Is motionless without comparison.
Naked and brittle as a wave, as I
Run through the water I can hear the sound
Of running echoed back and forth again across the beach—
My flesh.

A PRAYER FOR PVT. GRAHAM MACKINTOSH
ON HALLOWEEN

Infernal warlocks dressed in pink
And children wearing masks by night,
Protect my friend from sundry harm
And rest his body in your arms.

Ghosts of eternal silences
And pumpkin-faces wreathed in flame,
Consume the military flesh
Of those who borrow young men's lives.

You white-faced boys that trick or treat
And ring the doorbells of the dead,
Twist out each patriotic bone
Of those that consummate the loan.

And have the nasty little girls
Who steal the seed from dead men's loins
Make pee-pee on their uniforms
And dance on their conscripted flag.

Avenge for him this Hallows Eve
Each moment of captivity.
Let every ghost of liberty
Parade before him in his sleep.

Infernal warlocks dressed in pink
And children wearing masks by night,
Protect my friend from sundry harm
And rest his body in your arms.

TO A CERTAIN PAINTER

There is a storm at the end of your eyes.
Paint falls through the air like rain, splashing
In and out of patterns. The ground is plunging
Back and forth in shining celluloid colors.

It is God's colored world and at his eye
Shape covers shape and color splashes color
Things move too fast, slop out and start again.
Reality is blowing on the howling wind
Through his kaleidoscope.

If you are a painter with pretty eyes
You can make things stop moving.
You can stop things moving
If you roll your eyes at them.
And you are in a room
And the colors knock upon the roof like rain
But you have hold of the end of the rainbow.
Or you can reach out the window
And catch a falling flash of lightning
And quiet it;
Stroking its jagged strength with easy fingers
As if it were a frightened puppy on your lap.

Big-eyed lover, you seduce what God watches.
You make vision touch you
Gently on the eyes like a kiss.
You rob every storm of its rainbow; every sight
Of its shape and color.
You are looking back at God with your eyes
Through his own kaleidoscope.

Besides, you have pretty eyes.

EPILOGUE IN ANOTHER LANGUAGE

Ze love I talk for you in poetry
Was in zat strange American
We used to speak
No romance language zat, mon cher,
Zat was ze heart. (He is a crazy beast
he speak so strange.)
But now, mon cher, we have a better tongue
Ze heart has made no noise
He seldom beat.
When I see you and talk, ze heart, zat beast
I, how you say
Dead.

A POEM FOR DADA DAY AT THE PLACE

April 1, 1955

Darling,
The difference between Dada and barbarism
Is the difference between an abortion and a wet dream.
An abortion
Is a conscious sacrifice of the past, the painting of a mustache
On Mona Lisa, the surrender
Of real children.
The other, darling, is a sacrifice
Of nobody's children, is barbarism, is an Eskimo
Running amok in a museum, is Bohemia
Renouncing cities it had never conquered.
An ugly Vandal pissing on a statue is not Phidias
Pissing on a statue. Barbarism
Is something less than a gesture.
Destroy your own gods if you want Dada:
Give up your vices, burn your jukebox,
Draw mustaches on music, paint a real mother
On every non-objective canvas. Befoul only
Those things that belong to you.
"Beauty is so rare a thing," Pound said,
"So few drink at my fountain."
You only have the right to piss in the fountain
If you are beautiful.

AN ANSWER TO A JEW

When asked if I am of the Jew or Goyim,
When asked if I am an enemy of your people,
I would reply that I am of a somewhat older people:
The Gay, who are neither Jew nor Goyim,
Who were cut down in your Lord God Jehovah's first pogrom
Out at Sodom.
None of the nations ever protested about it
(We should never have nationalized angels) but show us
An angel again
Walking down Sodom St., wings folded,
And try us.

MANHATTAN

The horror of this city. Stone piled on stone,
Dollar on dollar, cloud upon cloud!
The little Jewfaced children
Playing in the deep streets.

[August 7, 1955]

THE PANTHER
(from Rilke's *Neue Gedichte*)

His jungle eyes have grown so tired watching
Each bar that they are impotent and sore.
They seem to see a thousand bars around them—
Beyond those bars, behind them, nothing more.
His body turns and turns in quiet circles
Subduing savage tension in its stride.
It seems a dance of strength around a center
At which, bemused, a captive witness rides.
But even now a door within the eyeball
Slides softly out, then something he can see
Comes through the iron stillness of his body,
Reaches his heart, and ceases there to be.

[THESE WOODS, SO FIT FOR EMPERORS]

These woods, so fit for emperors, reveal
A thousand detailed alleys where we feel
Each other waiting.
Believe these royal woods, remember them.
Where we have never been is real.

CENTRAL PARK WEST

Along the walks the sweet queens walk their dogs
And dream of love and diamonds as they pass
And I could be a statue or a stone
As they walk by me dreaming of their gods.
Beside their path, an apple's throw away,
I see that old erotic garden where
Our parents breathed the wasteful, loving air
Before the angry gardener changed his will.
The park has no room for that memory.
Its paths are twisted like a scattered sky
Of foreign stars. The spinning queens go by
Within their orbits, leaving me alone.
What cosmic joy. The last companion here
Is Priapus, the gardener's ugly son
Who crouches in the bushes with his shears
And hasn't got the hots for anyone.

[AND NO ONE IS AROUND TO SEE MY TEARS] *

And no one is around to see my tears
But Priapus, the ugly gardener's son,
Who squats among the flowers with his shears
And doesn't have the hots for anyone.

*Sent on a postcard to Allen Joyce, July 16, 1955.

HIBERNATION — AFTER MORRIS GRAVES

Deeper than sleep, but in a room as narrow
The mind turns off its longings one by one,
Lets beautiful black fingers snap the last one,
Remove the self and lie its body down.
The Future chills the sky above the chamber.
The Past gnaws through the earth below the bed.
But here the naked Present lies as warmly
As if it rested in the lap of God.

PORTRAIT OF AN ARTIST

Ovid among the Thracians soon received
A willing smile from those who baked his bread;
Walked country highways thinking of the dead;
Was nodded at by strangers as he grieved.

Not at Colonus, speaking sacred words
But cunning, exile, silence—country things.
As winter came he watched familiar birds
Fly southwards toward the sea on little wings.

THE DAY FIVE THOUSAND FISH DIED
ALONG THE CHARLES RIVER

And when the fish come in to die
They slap their heads against the rocks until they float
Downstream on one dead eye. From rocks
The Irish boys yell and throw rocks at them and
    beat them with their sticks.
Gulls wheel in the fine sky. Tall as an ogre
God walks among the rocks. His angels cry,
"Yell and throw rocks at them and beat them
    with sticks!"
But watch those upturned eyes
That gleam like God's own candles in the sun. Nothing
Deserves to live.

SONG FOR THE GREAT MOTHER

One minute after midnight, Mrs. Doom
From the middle distance of another room
Begins to take the furniture apart
And close the drawers, and slam the windows shut.
She puts away each angry, loving sight
We left behind us or had heard or touched.
She rolls the carpet up on which we danced
Sweeps up the dust, then sighs and snaps the light.
And if we sleep, she whispers round our beds
And buzzes at the corners of our eyes
Snipping each dream with hungry murmuring.
Oh, who would take this darkness for his bride?
Nothing is changed by her. All things remain
As beautiful and angry as they were.
She merely wipes their shadows from our hearts,
Shakes out her broom, and shuts the final door.

[1956]

FIVE WORDS FOR JOE DUNN
ON HIS TWENTY-SECOND BIRTHDAY

I shall give you five words for your birthday.
The first word is *anthropos*
Who celebrates birthdays.
He is withered and tough and blind, babbler
Of old wars and dead beauty.
He is there for the calmness of your heart as the days race
And the wars are lost and the roses wither.
No enemy can strike you that he has not defeated.
No beauty can die in your heart that he will not remember.

The second word is *andros*
Who is proud of his gender,
Wears it like a gamecock, erects it
Through the midnight of time
Like a birthday candle.
He will give you wisdom like a Fool
Hidden in the loins
Crying out against the inelegance
Of all that is not sacred.

The third word is *eros*
Who will cling to you every birthnight
Bringing your heart substance.
Whomever you touch will love you,
Will feel the cling of His touch upon you
Like sunlight scattered over an ancient mirror.

The fourth word is *thanatos,* the black belly
That eats birthdays.
I do not give you *thanatos.* I bring you a word to call Him
Thanatos, devourer of young men, heart-biter, bone-licker.
Look, He slinks away when you name Him.
Name Him! *Thanatos.*

The last word is *agape,*
The dancer that puts birthdays in motion.
She is there to lead words.
Counter to everything, She makes words
Circle around Her. Words dance.
See them. *Anthropos* ageless,
Andros made virgin, *Eros* unmirrored,
Thanatos devoured.
Agape, Agape, ring-mistress,
Love
That comes from beyond birthdays,
That makes poetry
And moves stars.

[1956]

BABEL 3

It wasn't the tower at all
It was our words he hated.
Once our words rose
Into God's willing mouth
Like bells sing into houses.
When someone loved
The word said love,
On the 38th floor,
On the 94th floor,
On the 1224th floor.
Words were different then. God didn't
Divide us into different languages
He divided
Words and men.
Men and words—He called the words angels.
We called the words angels.
Things were different then.

A POEM TO THE READER OF THE POEM

I throw a naked eagle in your throat.
I dreamed last night
That I was wrestling with you on the mountainside.
An eagle had a dream over our heads.
We threw rocks at him.
I dreamed last night—
This is false in any poem
Last night never happened
Couldn't
Make you feel the meaning so quickly
That I could tell you what I dreamed last night
That I could tell you that I dreamed I was wrestling
With the reader of this poem.
Dreamed—
Was it a wet dream?
Or dry
Like a dream is
When boys in a dream throw rocks at it?
I heard myself sobbing in a wet dream
Don't worry I will tell you everything.

I had a dream last night
That I was wrestling with you on the mountainside.
Was it a wet dream?
No I would tell you if it was a wet dream.
It was this poem
Us
I wrestled with you in this poem
And it was not a wet dream.

Then define
If you don't want to scare him out of the poem
Define
The dream
The wrestling
The lie
And in
What sweet Christ's name the eagle we were throwing rocks
    at was,
And why I love you so much
And why it was not a wet dream.

I can't deny
The lie.
The eagle was
God or Charles Olson
The eagle was men wrestling naked
Without the hope of men wrestling naked.
The eagle was a wet dream.

But the eagle in my throat says, "Jack,
How can you write a poem to the reader of a poem?
Even in a dream you must love somebody."
This is another lie.
I did not wrestle with anybody
I wrestled with the reader of this poem.
Men kiss men
Not like anybody
Kisses a girl
Kiss each other like the map of Africa
Or a picture of a desert
Or a scale-map of the entire universe.

But this is not a wet dream.
We did not kiss each other.
My darling, if you flew
A naked eagle in my throat
I'd shout, "Exactly!
When I said this was a poem to the reader
I wanted to dig a pitfall
Only you could fall into.
You
Know who you are
Know how terribly far
From last night you are.
If I am old when you read this,
If I am dead when you read this,
Darling, darling, darling,
It was last night
When I wrestled with you.
I am wrestling with you.
It was not a wet dream or you would be wrestling
With a naked gravestone."

Take it simply
Suppose we had been exploring
The hills and canyons of hell
And wrestled
And fucked
And—Hell,
Nothing but a spoiled camping trip.
Wrestling! It was as if we were in a room full
Of faceless comedians.

That wasn't what I wanted to say. I wanted to
     tell you
That there is innocence too
And the blind grandeur
Of the face of a mountain
In all we would have surveyed
If it had been a wet dream
If we had traveled
Mapless, past what either of us knew
past the dead eagle,
Past the faceless comedians
Who bug us,
Past the past that has misplaced us,
Past all the dead lines in a poem that after all
Are only dead lines in a poem,
To the mountains
Where our hearts are
Where the heart is.
A wet dream—
I'll tell God
It was a wet dream.

SONG FOR BIRD AND MYSELF

I am dissatisfied with my poetry.
I am dissatisfied with my sex life.
I am dissatisfied with the angels I believe in.
 Neo-classical like Bird,
 Distrusting the reality
 of every note.
 Half-real
 We blow the sentence pure and real
 Like chewing angels.

"Listen, Bird, why do we have to sit here dying
In a half-furnished room?
The rest of the combo
Is safe in houses
Blowing bird-brained Dixieland,
How warm and free they are. What right
Music."
 "Man,
 We
 Can't stay away from the sounds.
 We're *crazy,* Jack
 We gotta stay here 'til
 They come and get us."

Neo-classical like Bird.
Once two birds got into the Rare Book Room.
Miss Swift said,
"Don't
Call a custodian
Put crumbs on the outside of the window
Let them
Come outside."

Neo-classical

The soft line strains
Not to be neo-classical.
But Miss Swift went to lunch. They
Called a custodian.
Four came.
Armed like Myrmidons, they
Killed the birds.
Miss Munsterberg
Who was the first
American translator of Rilke
Said
"Suppose one of them
Had been the Holy Ghost."
Miss Swift,
Who was back from lunch,
Said
"Which."

    But the poem isn't over.
    It keeps going
    Long after everybody
    Has settled down comfortably into laughter.
    The bastards
    On the other side of the paper
    Keep laughing.
    LISTEN.
    STOP LAUGHING.
    THE POEM ISN'T OVER. Butterflies.
I knew there would be butterflies
For butterflies represent the lost soul
Represent the way the wind wanders
Represent the bodies
We only clasp in the middle of a poem.

See, the stars have faded.
There are only butterflies.
Listen to
The terrible sound of their wings moving.
Listen,
The poem isn't over.

Have you ever wrestled with a bird,
You idiotic reader?
Jacob wrestled with an angel.
(I remind you of the image)
Or a butterfly
Have you ever wrestled with a single butterfly?
Sex is no longer important.
Colors take the form of wings. Words
Have got to be said.
A butterfly,
A bird,
Planted at the heart of being afraid of dying.
Blow,
Bird,
Blow,
Be,
Neo-classical.
Let the wings say
What the wings mean
Terrible and pure.

    The horse
    In Cocteau
    Is as neo-classical an idea as one can manage.
    Writes all our poetry for us
    Is Gertrude Stein

Is God
Is the needle for which
God help us
There is no substitute
Or the Ace of Swords
When you are telling a fortune
Who tells death.
Or the Jack of Hearts
Whose gypsy fortune we clasp
In the middle of a poem.

"And are we angels, Bird?"
"That's what we're trying to tell 'em, Jack
There aren't any angels except when
You and me blow 'em."

So Bird and I sing
Outside your window
So Bird and I die
Outside your window.
This is the wonderful world of Dixieland
Deny
The bloody motherfucking Holy Ghost.
This is the end of the poem.
You can start laughing, you bastards. This is
The end of the poem.

[1956]

SOME NOTES ON WHITMAN FOR ALLEN JOYCE

"Let shadows be furnished with genitals."

He was reaching for a world I can still remember. Sweet and painful. It is a world without magic and without god. His ocean is different from my ocean, his moon is different from my moon, his love (oh, God the loss) is different from my love.

In his world roads go somewhere and you walk with someone whose hand you can hold. I remember. In my world roads only go up and down and you are lucky if you can hold on to the road or even know that it is there.

He never heard spirits whispering or saw Aphrodite crawl out of the water or was frightened by the ghost of something crucified. His world had clouds in it and he loved Indian names and carried some of his poems in a pouch around his neck. He had no need of death.

Rimbaud without wings.

Forgive me Walt Whitman, you whose fine mouth has sucked the cock of the heart of the country for fifty years. You did not ever understand cruelty. It was that that severed your world from me, fouled your moon and your ocean, threw me out of your bearded paradise. The comrade you are walking with suddenly twists your hand off. The ghost-bird that is singing to you suddenly leaves a large seagull dropping in your eye. You are sucking the cock of a heart that has clap.

Calamus cannot exist in the presence of cruelty. Not merely human cruelty, but the cruelty of shadows, the cruelty of spirits. Calamus is like Oz. One needs, after one has left it, to find some magic belt to cross its Deadly Desert, some cat to entice one into its mirror. There Walt is, like some great seabird from the Emerald Palace, crying, "Calamus, Calamus." And there one is, at the other side of the desert, hearing Walt but seeing that impossible shadow, those shimmering heat waves across the sky. And one needs no Virgil, but an Alice, a Dorothy, a Washington horsecar conductor, to lead one across that cuntlike mirror, that cruelty.

So when I dreamed of Calamus, as I often did when I touched you or put my hand upon your hand, it was not as of a possible world, but as a lost paradise. A land my father Adam drove me out of with the whip of shadow. In the last sense of the word—a fairy story. That is what I think about Calamus. That is what I think about your damned Calamus.

HOKKU

Big, up there
Goddess, they call her
Where in my room do the fish lie
Breathing out of their gills, naked, out of water
Out of any water, God-
Dess where the fish are plunging
Back and forth where there is nothing but sur-
Face.

Past
Remembering
(Torsos stored in a basement) Germane
To an issue.
A big flower
A pot
A seed

Loving you
My poetry said things I don't know.
Now
My poetry tries to heal me.
So im-
Personal, so loving
That poetry can cover both of us like a big
Blank-
Et.

Bitterness
Bitter - ness
People worry more about bitter than they worry about -ness
Worry more about -ness,
Damn you.

It is time to clean my house
Bare walls will attract pictures
Empty shelves paper
It is like a ruined lawn with snow on it
Something besides what has
Been beautiful.

Sure
Eurydice is dead
In hell or whatever
Black rope she is tied to.
Rimbaud was constructed by forty tinsmiths
Fifty balloonists
No one was ever/able/either.

LAST HOKKU

I don't like dreams where a right sound
Can put a minor emotion in amber. I mean the
        mirror
Where it is is there and anybody can thickly walk
        into it
I am sick of the right word and the poets
I have tried to teach the right word. There
In the old mirror, non-

Dissolving. Beautiful. I can't mean the

Right word. Trick yourselves, myselves in
Mirror.

JACOB

He had sent his family across the river.
The wives, the heavy oxen—paraphernalia
Of many years of clever living.
The water flowed past them. All that evening
Jacob was wrestling in the arms of a stranger.
It was not unexpected. By midnight
They had explored each other's strength and every hour
       was a tender repetition.
At dawn the angel tried to free himself and Jacob
Held him with one last burst of strength, screaming.
After that there had never been an angel. Lucky Jacob
Limped across the river, thinking of his wives and oxen.

EPILOGUE FOR JIM

The buzzards wheeling in the sky are Thanksgiving
Making their own patterns
There in the sky where they have left us.
It is hot down here where they have left us
On the hill or in the city. The hell
Of personal relations.
It is like a knot in the air. Their wings free
Is   there (our) shadows.

[DOWN TO NEW BEACHES]

Down to new beaches where the sea
More carefully than use-
Ual draws wild blue fish apart from its bottom froze-
N (or un-frozen) on the tides where we stand.
I mean, of course, poetry
And
Where the beach is too long for us
We gather.

[THE SLOBBY SEA]

The slobby sea where you float in
Has nothing but the edge of the water
I love
Your silence, your weakness, your pain
It is
(For each of us)
As if a single sea bird from the sky landed

OCTOBER 1, 1962*

This is an ode to Horace Stoneham and Walter O'Malley.
Rottenness.
Who has driven me away from baseball like a fast car. Say
It isn't true Joe.
This is an ode to John Wieners and Auerhahn Press
Who have driven me away from poetry like a fast car. Say
It isn't true Joe. The fix
Has the same place in junkie talk or real talk
It is the position
They've got you in.
The Giants will have a National League playoff. Duncan
Will read his poems in Seattle.
Money (I forgot the story but the little boy after it all was
        over came up to Shoeless
Joe Jackson) Say it isn't true Joe.

I have seen the best poets and baseball players of our
        generation caught in the complete and contemptible
        whoredom of capitalist society
Jack Johnson
At last shaded the sun from his eyes
                                    . A fix
You become fixtures like light
Balls. Drug
Habit
Walter O'Malley, Horace Stoneham, do you suppose
        somebody fixed Pindar and the Olympic Games?

*According to *Manroot #10,* this poem was tacked on the wall of
Gino & Carlo's Bar and copied on a brown paper bag by Lew Ellingham.

THREE MARXIST ESSAYS

HOMOSEXUALITY AND MARXISM

There should be no rules for this but it should be simultaneous if at all.

Homosexuality is essentially being alone. Which is a fight against the capitalist bosses who do not want us to be alone. Alone we are dangerous.

Our dissatisfaction could ruin America. Our love could ruin the universe if we let it.

If we let our love flower into the true revolution we will be swamped with offers for beds.

THE JETS AND MARXISM

The Jets hate politics. They grew up in a fat cat society that didn't even have a depression or a war in it. They are against capital punishment.

They really couldn't care less. They wear switchblade knives tied with ribbons. They know that which runs this country is an IBM machine connected to an IBM machine. They never think of using their knives against its aluminum casing.

A League Against Youth and Fascism should be formed immediately by our Party. They are our guests. They are ignorant.

THE JETS AND HOMOSEXUALITY

Once in the golden dawn of homosexuality there was a philosopher who gave the formula for a new society—"from each, according to his ability, to each according to his need."

This formula appears in the New Testament—the parable of the fig tree—and elsewhere.

To continue the argument is fruitless.

[1963?]

[BE BRAVE TO THINGS] *

Be brave to things as long as
As long as
As long as the plot thickens
As long as you hold a tiny universe in your
      hand made of stringy oil, cats' hair,
      tobacco, remnants
Of what was once wide,
As it was once as long as, the plot thickens.
      Be brave to thinkers in the night, rusted
      boxes, anything
That has dimension.
As if it were a foot wide
Tall, square, as long as boxes
Were

*Submitted to the Valentine contest of *Open Space* magazine,
February 1964.

THE POET AND POETRY — A SYMPOSIUM

The opinions of several poets as to the most interesting problems in writing poetry. Included in this symposium are: Robert Duncan, William Everson, Rosalie Moore, Jack Spicer, Leonard Wolf. [*Occident,* Fall 1949.]

JACK SPICER

Here we are, holding a ghostly symposium—five poets holding forth on their peculiar problems. One will say magic: one will say God; one will say form. When my turn comes I can only ask an embarrassing question—"Why is nobody here? Who is listening to us?"

Most of us are rather good poets. If we were actors or singers or cartoonists of the same relative talent, a sizeable percentage of the students of this University would recognize our names and be familiar with our work. As it now stands, I doubt if there is a reader of this magazine (including the editorial staff and the poets themselves) who is familiar with the work of all five poets. Yet, I repeat, there is not one of us that has not been recognized as a good poet by critics, magazines, or publishers.

The usual answer to this complaint, given, to use a homegrown example, in the letter column of the *Daily Californian* every time a new issue of *Occident* comes out, is so much hogwash: "Modern poetry does not make sense," the letter writer will passionately exclaim, "Nobody reads it because nobody understands it."

That is just not true. If a lack of intelligibility makes a work unpopular with the public, why is it that there is always at least one song with nonsense lyrics near the top of the Hit Parade? "Chickery Chick" was far less capable of prose analysis than *Finnegans Wake* and no one can claim that its bare, monotonous tune was responsible for its popular favor.

As a matter of fact recently some of the same people that condemn modern poetry as unintelligible express (weirdly enough) admiration for Edith Sitwell and Gertrude Stein. The phonograph records of *Facade* and *Four Saints in Three Acts* have made two writers (who are hardly paragons of intelligibility) perfectly acceptable to a large audience. What this audience has found is not the intelligibility that it had modestly asked for, but that greater boon that it did not dare to ask—entertainment.

The truth is that pure poetry bores everybody. It is even a bore to the poet. The only real contribution of the New Critics is that they have demonstrated this so well. They have taken poetry (already removed from its main source of interest—the human voice) and have completed the job of denuding it of any remaining connection with person, place and time. What is left is proudly exhibited in their essays—the dull horror of naked, pure poetry.

Live poetry is a kind of singing. It differs from prose, as song does, in its complexity of stress and intonation. Poetry demands a human voice to sing it and demands an audience to hear it. Without these it is naked, pure, and incomplete —a bore.

If plays were only printed and never acted, who would read them? If songs were only printed on song sheets, who would read them? It would be like playing a football game on paper. Do you wonder where the audience is?

It affects the nature of the poetry too. There was a time in the middle ages when music was mainly written and not sung. It was a time when crab canons were composed, complicated puzzles made of notes that no ear would think of hearing. Poetry, when it is removed from a living audience, loses its living form, becomes puzzling. It becomes blind like the salamanders that live in dark caves. It atrophies.

Orpheus was a singer. The proudest boast made about

Orpheus was not that his poems were beautiful in and of themselves. There were no New Critics then. The proudest boast was that he, the singer with the songs, moved impossible audiences—trees, wild animals, the king of hell himself.

Today we are not singers. We would rather publish poetry in a little magazine than read it in a large hall. If we do read in a hall, we do not take the most elementary steps to make our poetry vivid and entertaining. We are not singers. We do not use our bodies. We *recite* from a printed page.

Thirty years ago Vachel Lindsay saw that poetry must connect itself to vaudeville if it was to regain its voice. (Shakespeare, Webster and Marlowe had discovered this three centuries before him.) Our problem today is to make this connection, to regain our voices.

We must become singers, become entertainers. We must stop sitting on the pot of culture. There is more of Orpheus in Sophie Tucker than in R. P. Blackmur; we have more to learn from George M. Cohan than from John Crowe Ransom.

INDEX OF TITLES AND FIRST LINES

Titles of poems are given in italic type

Grey Fox Books